Also by the Author

The Little Book of Awareness

The Quiet Place Within

Talks With Temerlen

Transforming Negative Emotions

The Heart of Awareness

author@pantheonprosebooks.com

A dialogue about body, mind, ego and awareness

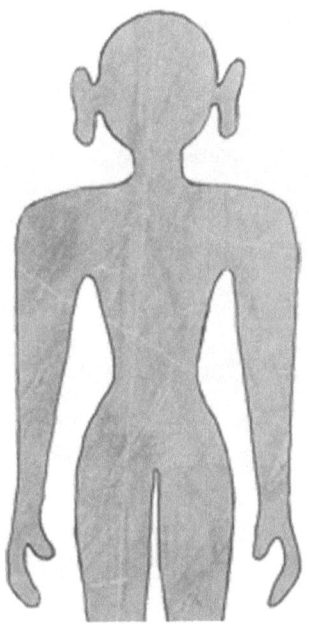

This Mystery and I

Advanced insights
for experienced seekers

Peter Ingle

This Mystery and I

Copyright © 2022 by Peter Ingle

All Rights Reserved

No part of this publication may be reproduced, store, or transmitted, in any form, or by any means, electronic, mechanical, photocopying, recording, or otherwise, without permission in writing from the author.

Library of Congress Cataloging-in-Publication Data

Ingle, Peter M.
This Mystery and I

ISBN: 978-1-7367425-1-8

Produced in the United States

cover art and design by
Olivia Ingle

Foreword

In response to my previous books, readers were asking to organize a series of gatherings to learn more about how I was combining ideas from non-dualism and the fourth way. A small group eventually met for several question-and-answer sessions which were recorded and edited for publication as this book. What follows is a dialogue about how body, mind, and ego contribute to our sense of 'I' and how this relates to the self-realization of awareness.

As ideas about enlightenment have become more popular, it has become easier to misconstrue enlightenment as an experience that happens to 'me' the person becoming more enlightened, more mindful, more awake. Bringing together ideas from non-dualism and the fourth way helps explain the cause of this psychological pitfall, how to recognize it, and how to circumvent it.

The book's title, *This Mystery and I*, was inspired from a line in Walt Whitman's poem 'Song of Myself' which can be understood in two ways at the same time: that body, mind, and ego come to be a stranger to awareness while, conversely, the egoic 'I' purported by body, mind, and ego can never comprehend the mystery of awareness which is wordless, formless, and timeless.

The discussion on these pages does its best to convey what awareness *is*, but that necessarily remains an elusive goal. As G.I. Gurdjieff said, "Man cannot explain what he himself really is." This is because awareness is a higher dimension that is incomprehensible to the body and mind and to the ego they foster. At best, the body and mind can intuit the flavor of awareness, learn to recognize some of its traces, and deduce what it is *not*. The more this happens, the more awareness comes to realize itself as the consciousness of itself.

In that spirit, this book is not really intended for you the reader. It is a message from awareness to awareness, delivered by one person to another person in the hope that 'you' will decipher the message and discern its true content.

This Mystery and I

I and this mystery,
here we stand.

Walt Whitman

This Mystery and I

Monterey, California

Fall 2021

I would like to better understand what the ego is and how it operates as our identity.

The ego is a psychological hologram that the mind projects every few seconds as a sense of 'I'. This hologram bends and twists and takes on different colors according to the situation. As a result, we project a slightly different persona at work, another at home, another at dinner parties, another when we meet strangers. We look the same, but our sense of 'I' and our projection of 'I' changes. To understand why the ego does this, you have to understand it in relation to awareness.

Whereas the ego is your feeling of 'I' and 'me', awareness is your consciousness of this sense of 'I'. But this consciousness is not usually aware of *itself*, and because of this it unwittingly attaches itself to what it perceives. When it attaches to thoughts and emotions, the mind uses this attachment to project the ego.

The more awareness attaches to your mind, the more it loses consciousness of itself and the more it strengthens your feeling of identity as a person. This is why attachment is also called identification, although it is more accurate to say that attachment ends up as identification.

Where does the feeling of 'I' reside?

In between awareness and the mind there is a thin membrane. Over time, the ego accumulates in this membrane as an image of 'I'. The mind projects the image of 'I' into the membrane where it leaves an imprint, almost like a developed photograph. But because awareness is not conscious of itself, and because the membrane is transparent, awareness does not distinguish between itself and the image of 'I' in the membrane. It thinks it is the hologram. Only when awareness brings *itself* into focus does the distinction become clear.

But the ego comes from somewhere, doesn't it?

We are not born with an ego. It is not a natural part of who and what we are when we are born. It accumulates during our life as a by-product of awareness repeatedly identifying with our thoughts, emotions, and sensations. After just a few years as a human being, this accumulation molds the foundation of a sense of 'I'. By the age of six or seven, most children have a well established ego. After that, their sense of 'I' grows stronger and the membrane housing the ego gets more opaque until awareness no longer shines through as itself.

What happens to the ego in enlightenment?

Because the ego is just a hologram, it evaporates under the light of conscious awareness. If the light is strong enough, it completely absorbs the image of 'I' and the image disappears. As this happens, the membrane that housed the ego becomes transparent again and the mind returns to being simply an instrument absent of identity. Awareness prevails as the conscious realization that it is pure awareness.

Can you say more about the membrane of the ego?

It is just a description, an analogy. But we can say that near the back wall of the mind there is a thin membrane where the ego accumulates as a sense of 'I'. Due to the transparency of this membrane, the ego and awareness mistake themselves for each other. Awareness thinks it is 'I' and 'I' thinks it is awareness. The question, "Who am I?" forms in this membrane. The self-realization of awareness happens on the other side of it.

How does identification come into play?

Identification acts as an electric current that cauterizes awareness to the mind and body. It transfers unconscious awareness to the mind and body where it is appropriated as a feeling of 'I'. With self-realization, this energy returns to awareness and the feeling of 'I' dissipates.

You can also think of identification as an electric cable. By means of this cable, the energy of awareness attaches itself to whatever it perceives. If you reverse the flow of energy in the cable, it returns to awareness and awareness becomes aware of itself as pure perception.

A good way to notice identification is in the form of momentum. You can't stop moving or talking or emoting or eating. Identification has absorbed you in its flow. The opposite happens when momentum gets broken, such as when you get ill or injured or suffer loss. You suddenly find yourself more established in presence. The next step is then whether presence becomes aware that it is present.

You said attachment ends up as identification. Aren't they basically the same thing?

Attachment is the beginning of identification. Awareness starts to attach itself to something and then it sticks. It becomes identified with it. At that point awareness either puts its identity in the thing and believes it is that thing, or it imbues the thing with an identity of its own. An example of the first instance is when awareness takes itself to be a thought or emotion or sensation or action. An example of the second instance is when awareness believes that an object or person or event is more significant than its awareness of it. In both cases awareness loses itself in the object it perceives.

Does it make a difference what we get identified with?

It makes no difference. It is still identification. The form it takes is secondary. What is important to understand is how identification happens and how it affects awareness. For example, some people are identified with their bodies and beards and hair. Other people are identified with their clothes and cars. Others are identified with food or money or family, or with politics or health or the environment. Everyone is constantly identified with one thing or another. We identify with each thought, each feeling, each opinion, each activity, each project. Our life becomes a series of one identification after another and it all happens at the expense of awareness.

A good example of identification is mobile phones. It is easy to see that people are identified with their phones, immersed in the screen, always holding the phone, even while driving. They feel comforted by having it with them and they feel anxious without it. It is also apparent when a person's awareness disappears into 'phone zone'. They do not see anything else and often do not hear anything that is said to them. It is equally apparent when their awareness emerges from the phone. You can see the light returning to their eyes.

The truth, however, is that people are not addicted to their phones as much as they are addicted to their ego. The phone is merely an enabler. The ego feels important just to be seen talking on the phone. It also loves social media because the ego is all about how it is perceived by other egos and how it compares to others. It thrives in the arena of appearance, recognition, status, and reputation. With a phone it can indulge in this arena even while sitting alone at home. In this sense, identification is not just physical and psychological. It has become electronic. Identification has morphed into electronification.

Can we see the hologram of the ego?

You don't see a visual image, but you can feel it behind your thoughts because the main thing that gives the ego shape are the thoughts and feelings generated by the mind. These are then reinforced by more thoughts and feelings in a self-perpetuating wheel that grinds a sense of identity into the psyche. Look behind your thoughts, feelings, and sensations. Notice the feeling of 'me' lurking in their shadow. Learn to distinguish this feeling from your ability to be aware of it. The more you do this, the more visible the ego becomes. Instead of it feeling like 'you', it starts to feel like a gremlin living inside the field of awareness.

You can also see the ego by studying identification in yourself. When awareness gets identified, there is turbulence in the mind and body. We feel proud, anxious, boastful, flustered, zealous, frantic, hurried, afraid, upset, angry. All of these reactions are the ego being boosted positively or negatively and taking on different shapes accordingly.

Is the ego more pronounced when we are upset and angry?

It is more pronounced the more identified we are. For instance, when we feel proud. But it also gains intensity through negativity because our instinctive energy is then behind it full throttle. When you see yourself or someone else expressing negative emotions, you are seeing the result of awareness identifying itself with the mind and body and *becoming* the ego. As identification increases, the ego gets stronger and negativity gets more intense.

Negative emotions, however, are not the ego. They are byproducts. The mind and body act as a conduit for negative emotions and the ego uses negative emotions as a club to fight with, a shield to protect itself with, and a cloak to disguise its phantom identity. When you take negative emotions away from the ego, it atrophies and a state of clear awareness starts to view you and your life in a new light.

Why does the ego exist in the first place?

It exists because awareness is not aware of itself. When awareness is unconscious it gets appropriated by the mind and body as a sense of identity that forms as the ego. But the mind and body can also be a medium through which awareness realizes itself as awareness. In both cases, the ego is the hinge. When identification prevails, this hinge swings in one direction and you live with the turmoil of identity as a person. When awareness prevails, the hinge swings in another direction and all the space that was filled with identity becomes an arena for pure awareness. The ego itself is an artificial growth in our psyche, but it is not bad. It is simply a matter of whether awareness is identified with it or not. What will it take for awareness to unplug itself from this socket and realize itself? This is our concern.

Can we recognize awareness in people?

Awareness can, but what it sees is not a mental or physical characteristic of the other person. What awareness sees in another person is awareness, or the absence of awareness, or the material of awareness caught up in a notion of 'I' in the person. Awareness can also see this about itself. It can see that it is starting to get entangled again in the identity of 'me'.

When you talk about awareness and consciousness, are you talking about one thing or different aspects of the same thing?

The words are interchangeable, with a slight distinction. Consciousness is the consciousness of things. Awareness is the consciousness of consciousness itself. As Jean Klein often said, we are too accustomed to thinking of ourselves in relation *to* things and being conscious *of* things. Seldom do we consider consciousness in relation to itself as pure awareness with no relation to anything else. Seldom do we consider the nature of awareness itself, its formlessness, its stillness and silence, its inherent mystery as pure perception.

When awareness starts to discover itself, you realize that everything which awareness is aware of is secondary. In the light of conscious awareness, your sense of identity as a person fades into the shadow.

Can the mind see awareness?

Awareness sees the mind, but the mind cannot see awareness because the mind cannot step out of the maze of its own mental concepts. When someone in whom awareness is conscious talks about awareness to someone in whom awareness is dormant, it inevitably gets interpreted on the level of mind and body. They look for evidence of it on their level, in their respective domains. They conclude that they should be able to see or hear or touch awareness in some way.

It is also true that as the mind hears about awareness, dormant awareness can pick up the scent of its own self-realization. This is the influence of awareness in one person loosening the shackles in the mind of another person, which is inferred in the story about the angel opening the prison door and the apostles walking out. What is interesting is that the angel only opened the door. They walked out by themselves.

Does the mind know when this happens?

The mind knows it is being affected in some way, but it does not know the awareness that moves through it and animates it. It is like a wind instrument which is unaware of the wind that makes it sing. The instrument does not know the wind. It knows only the music it makes.

Did you say that the question "who am I" comes from awareness?

I said it comes from the membrane between mind and awareness. But this is just an analogy to explain how it forms. The thought 'Who am I' springs from the mind and settles in this membrane as the feeling of being a person.

When this question poses itself in you, try to realize that it is just a thought. There is a subtle shift from being the sense of 'I' to being the awareness that sees 'I' having thoughts.

Awareness itself is always just out of reach of the mind and body. It is not tangible to them, but it is discernible to itself as a silent dimension of perception. It never asks, 'Who am I'? or 'What do I really want?' At best, these are the mind questioning itself or questioning awareness. The fact that the mind poses these questions demonstrates that it does not comprehend the nature of awareness. It thinks it wants to know awareness, but it cannot *be* awareness. Awareness can, however, make its presence known to the mind and the mind can then align with awareness. The primary way it aligns with awareness is by becoming quiet and yielding to the utter reality of circumstances.

So becoming quiet refers to the mind?

It can refer to both the mind and to awareness. When teachers say, "Just be quiet," they usually mean 'quieten the mind' so that the empty space in the mind can be available for awareness to realize itself. But the expression "Be quiet" can also be an imperative directed at awareness, imploring awareness to *be* the quiet stillness of itself and realize itself as that.

Is awareness in the present moment? Is this what it means to be present and in the moment?

It is the other way around. Awareness is not actually in the present moment. The present moment is in awareness. One way to think of it is that this moment *was* the future and *will be* the past, just as the past was the future and the future will be the past. Past, present, and future are mental concepts of time which all resolve in eternity as the same moment in awareness. 'Now' means that it is always this moment, which is how awareness sees it. So it is more accurate to say that the present moment is in awareness because it exists inside the field of awareness just as the past and future do.

This seems like a puzzle to the mind, but to awareness it is a simple reality. It is always now, and this now resides in awareness.

Surely time exists, though. We see things change over time. Out bodies age. New buildings appear. All of this happens in time and through time. Yes?

The body views time one way. The mind another way. And our emotions another way.

Each of these also experiences time at a different speed. So, yes, time does exist for them just as space exists for them. The situation is different in the dimension of awareness which is motionless, spaceless, and timeless.

When you realize that awareness is a different dimension of consciousness, you see that nothing which happens in the moment affects awareness. Whatever happens, it just happens and awareness just sees it. Everything keeps changing in front of awareness as awareness remains the same. In this sense, everything exists in its own time inside the timeless dimension of awareness. But the mind can never quite figure this out.

You hear athletes saying they are living in the moment as a way of enhancing their performance. Is this the same thing as being present?

It is easy to misinterpret the idea of being present as something that happens on the level of the mind and body. The misinterpretation is that we are physically passing through a series of moments, concentrating on each of them, and not racing to the next one. The actuality, however, is that awareness is not physical or psychological and that it is always standing still as the moment passes through its field of consciousness. Awareness does not experience a series of linear moments. It sees the same moment. The same flower keeps unfolding in different ways inside awareness.

You said awareness can make its presence known to the mind. In what way?

We cannot see the wind, but we can see how it acts on the world of physical objects. The human eye can also see water vapor precipitate as rain, but it cannot see water evaporate. Similarly, although the mind cannot see awareness, it can detect the influence of awareness on the mind and body. For instance, the mind can register the effect of identification and detect that awareness has collapsed out of itself and into identification. But it cannot see awareness when awareness rises as pure consciousness.

When we learn about awareness, the mind and body try to bend it into a shape they can understand, which they cannot. Meanwhile, awareness becomes conscious of itself behind everything, and increasingly conscious of how infinite this background is. The more the consciousness of awareness expands, the farther it extends into that background beyond the reach of the mind.

Nevertheless, a connection remains between the mind and awareness. For example, even though awareness does not speak, it can breathe impulses into the mind which the mind then vocalizes as thoughts. These inspired thoughts can seem like 'the voice of awareness', but they are only thoughts responding to impulses. Most thoughts do not spring from awareness this way, so it is important to distinguish between normal thoughts that spring directly from the mind and inspired thoughts which emerge indirectly as a result of awareness. Thoughts that are inspired—'breathed into' the mind—by awareness have a different measure of purity, clarity, and depth. But they are still only thoughts.

Do you recommend spiritual retreats as a way to strengthen spiritual practice?

Spiritual practice refers to the mind and body aligning themselves in support of awareness. Practice is scaffolding for awareness. For instance, when awareness is more conscious, you notice things more vividly, you are more settled in the moment, and you feel less identified. Your concerns about being somebody dissipate. When this level of awareness wanes, you can recognize that it has waned, and then you practice. You practice by trying to recreate the inner conditions that made that deeper awareness possible. Namely, by trying to be less identified and trying to notice what is in the moment without attaching yourself to it, whether it be thoughts and feelings or the circumstances you find yourself in.

The most simple practice is to be aware of being aware of what is right in front of you. Wherever you are, whatever you are doing, you notice what is around you and try to be aware that you are noticing it. This is not a new idea. Jesus said, "See (consciously notice) what is before you (in the moment) and what is hidden (awareness) will be revealed (will realize itself)."

Another form of practice is to notice things with appreciation. Jean Klein called it 'affectionate awareness' because it is more than just seeing. It is about appreciating the object while also appreciating the fact that you are aware of it. When awareness perceives itself while perceiving—when it realizes itself as perception—this transforms the seeing. It happens naturally when awareness is conscious, but you can also evoke it with the mind. This is the idea behind 'self-remembering' in the fourth way. It is a way of jump-starting awareness; of trying to enter awareness through the back door.

But it is important not to mistake spiritual practices for awareness. Awareness itself does not practice. It does not do anything other than perceive, which is why it is such a relief to return to pure awareness.

Going on a retreat can help you realize all this, however you may go on a retreat where you experience deep silence, stillness, and tranquility, yet fail to realize that awareness looms behind all of them, just as it looms behind the activity, noise, and pressure of everyday life. In the end, you cannot live your life on retreat. Your life and you as the person living it both have to be absorbed by awareness, which is what happens as awareness becomes conscious of itself.

Why is silence so useful?

The best way to answer this is to explore it with awareness. We generally think of silence as the absence of sound, just as we think of stillness as the absence of movement. Both imply emptiness. Yet that is how the mind perceives them. When you explore them with awareness you find otherwise. Neither is empty nor absent. They are both full and complete. But only awareness experiences them this way.

Silence is useful because the core of our being is silent as well as still. It is a void. But it is the void of consciousness itself. We usually notice the movement of sensations, the noise of thoughts, and the turbulence of emotions and conclude that they all tie to the central core of ourselves as 'I'. But this is because we are identified. When we cease to identify, awareness discovers itself at a much deeper level which is the void of pure consciousness where silence and stillness reign, not as phenomena but as being.

You said everything comes down to being identified or not. How is it possible to be less identified?

First you have to see what being identified implies about awareness. Simple identification starts when awareness is unaware of being aware, which means that it is unconscious of itself. When this happens, awareness devolves into an innocent form of fascination with what it perceives.

When identification is more extreme, awareness gets completely submerged in the object of its perception and either derives identity from the object or imbues the object with identity. For example, when awareness identifies with your thoughts, it becomes them and mistakes them as itself. It becomes the mind experiencing itself as a sense of 'I' and 'my' thoughts. Alternatively, when awareness identifies with other people or circumstances, it grants them identity, authority, power, and significance.

The fourth way teacher Peter Ouspensky talked about two stages of identification: the stage of becoming identified, and the stage when identification is complete. The more you observe the second stage, the more interested you become in catching the first stage as it develops so it will not enter the second stage. You want to catch it sooner and sooner until you arrive at the point where identification begins. At that point you are on the threshold of awareness itself.

Being less identified and remaining not identified is akin to keeping your balance while riding a bicycle. At first you keep losing your balance and falling. After awhile you learn how to adjust and keep going. You may wobble a lot at first, but eventually everything straightens out. This is also just an analogy. To remain unidentified means awareness remaining consciously aware in the dimension of itself.

Ouspensky said that consciousness and identification are opposite sides of the same coin. Did he mean we have to reverse identification?

He meant that when awareness is unconscious, it is on the verge of becoming identified. And conversely, when awareness is less identified, it is on the verge of becoming conscious. As you become less identified you become more aware, and as you become more aware you become less identified. They transmute into each other.

Does the effort to keep your balance come from the mind or from awareness?

You discover the answer to this by knowing that you are trying to be aware. There is a difference between trying to be aware and awareness itself. Trying to be aware is a push by the mind trying to initiate awareness. Awareness itself does not try to be aware. It simply realizes that it is awareness. From this realization an innate urge to sustain awareness emerges, but this comes as part of the realization of awareness, not as a push from the mind.

But isn't it helpful for the mind to give this push?

The mind can think about awareness, yet it can never know awareness and it can never be awareness because the mind cannot get out of the dimension of itself and into the dimension of awareness. This becomes more clear when you realize that they are different dimensions. They are like the ocean and the sky. One is bound to the earth. The other is not.

The irony is that awareness already is itself and needs only to realize itself. It does not need to push or force itself into being. The mind, however, plays an important role because it can generate attitudes in support of awareness. Certain attitudes can open the door to awareness, just as other attitudes can open the door for identification.

This property of attitudes deserves examination. For example, how is it that different arrangements of thought can ignite awareness or propel it into identification? What are these things called attitudes? What causes them to fold and unfold in ways that have such different influences over us? Can we control how they unfold? If so, how might we harness them for the sake of awareness? There is a lot of material here for discovery and experimentation.

Are you talking about positive thinking?

No. Positive thinking is a point of view from the positive half of the intellect, just as negative thinking is a point of view from the negative half of the intellect. The mind engages positive thinking in the hope of making you feel better. It uses positive thoughts to replace negative thoughts to get you to think optimistically rather than pessimistically. But neither optimism nor pessimism exist in awareness because awareness has no positive or negative half. Pure perception is perception with nothing added. Things are just seen as they are and the reality of this is very powerful.

The attitudes I referred to are more complex

than just positive or negative points of view. If you look behind a point of view you will find an attitude lodged in the ego. For example, I may think to myself that I don't like you because you upset me or humiliated me. The point of view is that you are an unpleasant person and I don't like you. Behind this point of view is the feeling that you hurt me. Behind both the point of view and the feeling of hurt is an attitude about myself: that I am always right, or that I don't deserve to be treated this way, or that people should respect me and not demean me. This attitude is like a current that perpetuates identification and negativity. It gives me permission to take things personally, feel hurt, and judge you. As long as the attitude remains in place, I am justified in getting upset and thinking poorly of you. This attitude also protects the ego because then I have no reason to question why I feel the way I do. I can just conclude that the problem is always with other people or with the situation.

But what if I could create a new attitude, not to think positively or feel better, but to help me not get identified when someone criticizes me or when things don't go my way? What if I could use the feeling of being attacked and hurt as a cue to notice the ego behind that feeling? What if I could do this with all my negative emotions—turn them around on themselves, and use them as flashlights to expose the imaginary 'I' of ego?

Developing this kind of thinking about your automatic attitudes can diminish identification and promote awareness. It is demanding work that requires more than just a positive outlook.

Byron Katie has a similar approach where she walks people through the attitudes that are making them suffer. She helps them see how their thinking is causing the suffering.

Yes. As her work demonstrates, seeing an underlying attitude for what it is can loosen identification and free awareness. The more you take yourself as a person out of the picture, the more the reality of the picture comes into focus. It is fascinating that a different attitude can lead us to reality. It shows how valuable the mind can be in self-realization.

The idea of attitudes is also described by Carol Dweck, a professor of psychology at Stanford. She wrote the book *Mindset* which talks about the difference between a growth mindset and a fixed mindset. She explains that a growth mindset is open yet comprises more than positive thinking, just as a fixed mindset is closed yet comprises more than negative thinking. You can apply her idea of mindsets on the level of the mind and see very good results. You see even better results when you understand how some attitudes open the door to awareness. This is powerful, almost mystical.

Different systems and teachings sometimes claim to be the best one. How can I distinguish between them and know which one is right for me?

Spiritual teachings exist to point the mind to something higher. What they point to is the same, but the way they guide the mind varies. Their limitation is that the mind tries to use them to form a conceptual framework of what is being pointed to, and then the mind ends up getting stuck in its own framework.

A credible teaching knows that the only way to breach the gap between the mind and awareness is for awareness to transmute from the realm of thoughts to the thoughtless dimension of pure consciousness. Awareness is entangled in the mind and transmutation involves slipping out of the mind and returning to itself. No thought or concept or mental effort can do that. Only awareness can slip out.

The choice of which teaching to study is a personal one, usually an intuitive one. It is safe to say that you will be most drawn to the one you are most ready for. The important thing to understand is that a teaching is just a reference guide. If you remember this, you won't get stuck on the wheel of trying to figure everything out in terms of ideas and definitions.

I understand a lot of what you are saying but I can't seem to get out of my mind. Even if I try to establish myself as the observer I get swept into the river of thoughts.

There is a deep-seated feeling that we need thoughts. Awareness keeps falling into them because it thinks it needs to be thinking. But it doesn't. It is only the mind that thinks that because the mind knows itself only as thoughts, which is like a room knowing itself only as furniture. The furniture is talking to itself and occupying all the attention in the room such that the empty space in the room no longer recognizes itself.

All you can do is try to back away from thoughts enough to realize that you are the space in the room. When you gain enough distance as the witness, it becomes clear that you are not in your thoughts. They are in you. At first the witness develops in your mind as a thought that sits on the river bank watching the other thoughts go by. Then awareness comes to realize itself as both the river bed and the river bank. It remains motionless as everything else passes through it, including the witness sitting on the river bank.

So the witness is not awareness?

From the perspective of the mind there seems to be a perceiver, an observer, a witness. From the perspective of awareness there is simply perceiving. There is no identity, no point of psychological solidity. Nisargadatta said the witness is like a drop of dew in which the light of the sun is reflected. It seems to be light, but it is just a reflection. The so-called witness in the mind is the same. It reflects awareness but it is not the source of awareness.

The mind seems driven to produce thoughts about anything and everything.

The mind automatically inserts thoughts between awareness and whatever awareness is perceiving. It then produces more thoughts about those thoughts in a chain of random thoughts that go on and on and on. The fourth way calls this 'imagination' to imply that it is nothing more than the uncontrolled wandering of the mind.

This imagination becomes such a habit that we get more interested in the thoughts we have about what we see than in the seeing itself. As soon as we see something, we lapse into imagination about it and stop seeing what is in front of us. We conclude that we are our thoughts about it. Too much emphasis is put on thinking about *what* we see. Not enough emphasis is placed on being aware *as* we see. At the core of our being, we are this seeing. We are not vision. We are perception itself.

I thought if I stopped believing my thoughts that they would stop.

It is not a matter of disbelieving them or trying to stop the stream of imagination. It is a matter of seeing clearly what is right here right now without succumbing to the whirlpool of thoughts about it. The thoughts continue but you don't get sucked in. It helps to know that we don't need thoughts as much as the mind thinks we do. The mind likes them because they provide psychological security.

When you look behind thoughts, you see that the structure of the mind itself is silent, but we usually notice only its contents: the running river of thoughts. The structure itself lies close to awareness. It is like the wall of the room full of furniture. The wall backs right up against awareness, which is why becoming aware of your thoughts can lead to awareness becoming aware of itself.

When you have trouble with thoughts, return to simply looking at them. Don't interfere with them. Don't invest yourself in them. Leave them alone. Step back and settle into your proper place as the field surrounding them. Nisargadatta said that when you walk down a crowded street you don't engage with every person you encounter. You just find your way between and keep walking. This is a good way to view thoughts. Don't engage them. Just keep walking. Or rather, stay still and let them keep walking. Allow yourself to fill the air around all of them.

But can I stop thoughts if I want to? Sometimes it feels like I can stop them.

The mind is what tries to stop thoughts. Awareness does not. It has no need to. It simply sees thoughts and knows it is seeing them, and that defuses them.

Any attempt to stop thought originates in the same dimension as thoughts themselves. This dimension is the mind and you step out of this dimension by noticing your thoughts and not identifying with them, by not becoming each thought. When you simply notice them, you give awareness a chance to intuit itself as a deeper dimension beyond thought. This is how awareness slips out of the mind and into itself.

Another way to envision this is to see that the space inside the mind can be filled with thoughts or with awareness. They displace each other. As one of them expands it pushes the other one out. In this sense, we can stop thought by filling the mind with awareness. For example, sit for a few minutes and try to notice everything around you. All the little things. Even the details in a blank wall next to you. Really notice them and simply be aware that you are noticing them. You will be astonished at how much you can see. You will also see how quickly thoughts intrude and try to reclaim that territory for themselves.

What changes when you reach that dimension? Does awareness think in its own way?

As we are, almost everything we perceive gets trapped in a filter of thought. Seldom does awareness know itself as pure seeing without thought. When you move past the mind's labels for things, everything in creation appears sacred because you see it directly. But awareness does not think about this because it does not think. It simply perceives, and this perceiving appreciates everything in a deeper way. It appreciates not only creation and our physical existence, but awareness itself, the fact that it exists, the mystery of its existence in the universe.

These deeper currents of awareness are hard

to explain. They are hinted at in poetry and art and music, but they can never find full human expression because the mind cannot plumb that depth. Science, which is an extension of the mind, tries to study awareness, but it cannot because it can study only things within its own dimension. It always tries to explain awareness as tangible matter, even matter at the quantum level. The truth, however, is that only awareness can study itself, and it does that by becoming increasingly aware of being aware.

The greatest mystery is to be aware of being the perception of all that exists. Most of what exists in the universe does not perceive this.

At dinner last night I heard you say that the mind is too slow to study awareness.

Yes. The mind, meaning the intellect, is the slowest part of our psychological machinery. The mind is like the earth. It does not register the sun. It just plods a slow predictable course, always in the same orbit. When the mind encounters an obstacle, it confronts it directly and struggles with it. Awareness does not struggle with things. It just sees them and embraces them, not as problems but as inevitabilities, as sources of energy, as catalysts. But there is no thinking about them. Awareness simply transforms everything into itself.

The mind cannot operate other than the way it does, and it is natural for the mind to derive satisfaction from its own mental activity. Incessant thought can be tantalizing, but it becomes less alluring as awareness discovers itself and realizes that it does not need to steep itself in the mind.

Can you talk about the mind's over-indulgence in thoughts and how this drives the ego?

The ego is a result of awareness losing consciousness of itself and burying its head in the sand of thoughts, emotions, sensations, and movement. This infuses a sense of 'I' into the mind and body. When awareness lifts itself out of this mire, the sense of 'I' is also withdrawn.

The mind plays the biggest role in our feeling of identity because the hologram of 'I' is generated in the mind and projected from there. Part of this projection is the urge to appear unique to others who, ironically, are embroiled in the same psychological complication on their side.

The mind immersed in thought and regulated by the ego thinks it is awareness until awareness realizes itself, which comes as a jolt.

Some teachers talk about the spiritual ego manifesting as enlightenment? Is this what you mean by the mind thinking it is awareness?

In general, the mind and body think they are aware. What you are asking about refers to the error that some people make of believing they as the person have become enlightened. This assumption stems from the instinctive side of the ego which tries to project a demeanor of presence. It is the body's way of trying to take ownership of awareness.

Awareness is not about the person or for the person. It is beyond. It does not aspire to demonstrate or prove or justify itself. Its simplicity stands in striking contrast to the complicated apparatus of the ego.

Whereas the ego thinks it is starring in its own movie, awareness is watching the movie. The ego wants other egos to think it is aware, but awareness is not concerned about that because it has no urgency of identity. It just floats in the background as perception.

Does the ego disappear when awareness self-realizes?

It is like a kernel of corn and popped corn. When self-realization pops, the awareness that was on the inside is turned outside, and the ego that was outside becomes a small point on the inside. It is still there as a remnant, but it is inconsequential.

Do animals have an ego?

Creatures in the animal, vegetable, and mineral kingdoms do not have a psychological identity. Their sense of aliveness derives only from their physical existence. Each animal, flower, and rock is unique, but none of them harbors a sense of 'I'. None of them compares itself to others or wants to be other than it is. None of them has negative emotions. None of them rejects its suffering. It is noteworthy, however, that awareness does not consciously realize itself through any of those life forms.

Sometimes you refer to the mind and body as the four lower centers. What do you mean?

This idea comes from the fourth way tradition which explains that instead of one brain we have four brains or four centers, each of which governs a specific realm of the mind or body. The four centers are called the instinctive, moving, emotional, and intellectual centers.

The instinctive center is the headquarters of our physiology and all our natural instincts such as breathing, digestion, coughing, regeneration of cells, immune system, nervous system, and so on. The primary concern of the instinctive center is safety, survival, and procreation.

The moving center governs all our movements such as walking, talking, reading, writing, riding a bike, typing, and manipulating tools. All movements that we have to learn are governed by this center. In many ways, the moving center also serves the instinctive center. It is literally the arms and legs of the instinctive center and because there is a close connection between these two centers they are sometimes referred to as one: as the instinctive-moving center.

In other teachings, the instinctive and moving centers are referred to as simply the body which includes the five senses. And what other teachings call the mind is explained in the fourth way as the emotional and intellectual centers.

The emotional center refers to the realm of all our emotions which include perceptions of people, nature, life forms, beauty. The emotional center does not move or think. It perceives emotionally, often at fast speed.

Then there is the intellectual center which processes information, ideas, theories, concepts, analysis, comparison, and logical thinking. This is the brain that generates the thoughts which vocalize in our head, although it also generates thoughts on behalf of the other centers. For example, the intellectual center will generate the instinctive thought, "I am hungry." Or the moving thought, "I better get up now." Or the emotional thought, "Those flowers are beautiful" or "I really like her."

Each of the four centers is independent of the others, but they are designed to operate together and to balance one another. For instance, behavior often starts as an impulse in the instinctive center which activates a response in the emotional center, which in turn prompts thoughts in the intellectual center and gestures in the moving center. The whole sequence unfolds within fractions of a second of the original impulse and we regard it as 'me'.

The sense of identity in each person also gravitates around the manifestations of the lower center that is predominate in them. For example, some people identify primarily with the sensory world, others with movement and projects, others with people and emotions, and others with ideas, information, and definitions.

Are they called lower centers because they are below awareness?

Yes. In a lower dimension. As I said, the idea of four centers is not mentioned in other teachings which usually refer to just the mind and body. The fourth way explains it in more detail and explains that the ego is a product of all four centers. It is a more complete breakdown of what we are as human beings.

The fourth way also describes awareness in terms of two higher centers—the higher emotional center and the higher intellectual center—to indicate the expansive nature of awareness. The higher emotional center equates to awareness realizing itself in a higher dimension. The higher intellectual center refers to awareness expanding into yet higher dimensions of itself.

The main idea is that the self-realization of awareness is not about the lower centers. Understanding what the lower centers are and how they operate helps you understand awareness. The more you realize what awareness is not, the more awareness realizes itself as awareness.

Ouspensky said that Gurdjieff referred to the lower centers as the four stories.

It was actually three stories. In Gurdjieff's analogy, each of the four centers has three levels or stories. Envision a house with four wings representing the four centers, and each wing has three floors. Each of the three floors or stories processes attention differently. The lower stories operate with little or no attention. The middle stories engage when their attention is drawn by something or to something. The upper stories come into focus when attention needs to be controlled. The higher the story, the higher the quality of attention it uses.

This breakdown of the four centers into stories helps you see that sometimes you do things without having to give much attention to them, while other things you do only when your attention is captivated. And there are some things you can do only when you carefully control attention. Using this framework you start to notice different levels of attention in yourself, and start to see which part of a center is operating and giving you a sense of 'I' in the moment.

But the most important thing is to realize that you can see all of the centers and different parts of centers as they operate. This seeing is awareness which looms behind all the centers but is normally unaware of itself watching them. It usually identifies with them and concludes that "this is me."

How is this better than studying ourselves in terms of just mind and body?

Behind each thought you will find a pulse of energy. Behind this energy is an impulse that gave rise to it. And behind the impulse is one of the four centers that generated it. Behind all of these is awareness. The more clearly you can distinguish all this in yourself, the better. For instance, you will see that your sense of 'I' is sometimes informed by the instinctive center, sometimes by the intellectual center, and other times by the emotional center. The ego is never the same 'I'. At different moments it comprises different 'I's and hides behind all of them.

The principle of four centers is not necessary, but it makes things more precise. When you can distinguish between the centers and between their manifestations and awareness, you will not be fooled so easily. Knowing about the lower centers also helps you understand that there is never anything wrong with awareness. The problem is always a blockage in the pipes of the lower centers that prevents the flow of awareness. The more skilled you are as a plumber, the better your chances are of finding and clearing these blockages.

I mentioned earlier that the ego tries to feign awareness. What I was referring to is when the ego disguises itself behind the instinctive center and projects an aura of awareness that impresses other people's instinctive centers. This is just one example of how the psychological waters we are trying to cross are trickier, more multifaceted, and more unpredictable than people realize. Knowing about the four lower centers helps you navigate across them.

Can you give examples of some of the blockages that impede the flow of awareness?

The underlying blockage for everyone is identification. We live with an ongoing urge to identify and we develop the habit of becoming identified. We rationalize that we can't get anything done unless we identify with doing it. We feel obligated to identify with other people, with our own thoughts and feelings, with problems, with the future. We feel impotent if we don't become identified. Yet the reality is that identification means a collapse of awareness.

When awareness loses consciousness, it collapses into identification. It falls from a higher dimension of pure consciousness into the psychological dimension of thought and emotion, and from there to the physical realm of sensation and movement. As this happens, awareness gets entangled in our thoughts, emotions, sensations, and movements, and infuses in them the feeling of being a unique person.

Identification also causes other blockages. For example, some people identify with themselves as superior and conclude that the problem is always other people, with other people's inadequacies or incompetence, and that other people must be made to come around to the right way of doing things. This kind of thinking compounds itself and leads to a feeling of uniqueness and superiority.

The opposite occurs when a person concludes that they are inferior, that they are the problem. They criticize themselves at every turn while trying to be better, but they always fail to do so because they think they are inferior. It is just another way the ego builds an image of 'I'. Whether the ego develops as a sense of superiority or inferiority, or as simply uncaring, it uses negative emotions to form a protective layer—like a line of defense—around the feeling of 'me'. The ego does this because it feels that it needs to be in control. When it senses that it is losing control, it uses negative emotions to gain or regain or not lose control, or to show that it resents having lost control.

What exactly is the ego wanting to control?

Have you heard of William Glasser? He was a psychiatrist who wrote about what he termed choice theory. His central idea was that people who appear to be mentally ill are in many cases masking the ego's unhappiness at having lost control. For instance, he explained that you don't just become depressed. Instead, the ego chooses to depress, as he puts it, to camouflage the fact that it is not getting what it wants from the world, or that it is being treated by others the way it doesn't want to be. But rather than resisting or expressing its anger, it burrows into depression to protect the sense of 'me'.

Glasser further argued that shock treatment and medications never address the underlying psychological source—the ego. They only dull the biological symptoms. As a result, people remain in therapy and on strong medication for years and years, often for the rest of their lives, and the ego remains entrenched.

Glasser's ideas coincide with how the four centers operate and how negative emotions fortify the ego. For example, negative emotions also mask reality. They are like a drug the ego gives itself to avoid and deny the truth. The ego is addicted to the drug of negativity, and this addiction impedes awareness. And as Glasser pointed out, this is the ego's way of trying to establish some semblance of control over itself.

When you boil it down, you see that the ego is nothing more than a psychologically induced sense of identity. When this is jeopardized or threatened or taken away, the ego experiences an emptiness that it wants to cover up or avoid. Doing either is its way of taking control again.

From this point of view, most of what we call normal behavior, including negative emotions, is actually abnormal. The ego, which is not a natural part of who we are when we are born, is abnormally desperate to maintain an illusion of 'me'. The option of facing the emptiness inside and yielding to it is simply not an option.

Negative emotions seem like waste matter rather than blockages. More like letting off steam than blocking the flow.

Negative emotions are not as harmless as they seem, but you realize this only by seeing their connection to awareness. Why are negative emotions harmful? Because they burn energy that belongs to awareness. Once you express a negative emotion that energy is gone. This is why the concept of negative emotions holds a central place in the fourth way system. You hear it mentioned in other teachings, but it is not given special importance. It is not explained in detail and few tools are provided for neutralizing negative emotions. The fourth way is a notable exception to this.

Why do we feel obligated to become identified and can we train ourselves not to be identified?

Awareness circulates through the mind and body, which is normal. What is abnormal is when it attaches to them and gets appropriated by them as identity. Identification means that awareness has not only entered the lower centers but has divested itself as their sense of identity. This identity needs more and more identification to fuel itself, and identification becomes a habit.

The lower centers themselves cannot control identification itself because it is something that is happening to awareness. Awareness has to control itself, so you have to know what identification feels like and you have to understand that it erodes awareness. Initially, you find yourself identified. Later you are able to feel it starting but you don't get submerged by it. Gradually you recognize it at the point where it is about to start but your seeing it prevents it from starting. Awareness learns to hold onto itself and not get subsumed.

Is it simply a matter of not reacting?

It is a matter of not reacting with identification. Most human beings are reacting automatically through identification rather than acting consciously from awareness. This is due to being here on earth in human form in this solar system and galaxy. Just as gravity is the predominant universal law governing our physical life, identification is the predominant universal law governing our psychological life. Identification is the norm on earth. Refraining from it is the exception. When the fourth way talks about escaping, it means awareness slipping free from the law of identification. This is an enormous change. As this changes, many other things can change. It is like unlocking the treasure chest that has been confining awareness.

I would appreciate if you could give more examples of how the ego protects itself by hiding behind negative emotions.

Identification breeds the ego and the two of them together breed negative emotions. If you are not identified, you will not become negative. When you do become negative, look behind the negative emotion and you will find the phantom self of the ego. A negative emotion is evidence of the ego, but it does not want to be discovered at its root so it spews negativity the way an octopus spews ink to cover its tracks.

Spiritual teachers say the ego feeds off of turmoil. How do you understand this?

No matter how many comforts of life we have, the ego is never at ease for long because it maintains its profile through conflict with the world, with others, and with itself. It is identified with its idea of how all of these should be and it uses negativity to oppose them when they don't satisfy its idea. The ego can be positive at times, but it always turns to the negative because at its core it is negatively charged.

This makes sense when you realize that the ego is not a legitimate identity. It is a psychological tendency to establish identity through comparison, opposition, judgment, and so on. When we get identified, we fuel this tendency.

As identification intensifies, awareness precipitates into denser and denser forms of energy that coalesce as the ego. We can even say that the ego is a calcification of awareness brought about by identification. And the most calcified form is negative emotions. The ego doesn't get any more dense than that.

This is why the fourth way uses the non-expression of negative emotions as a focal point for exposing the imaginary 'I' of ego. It is a powerful method if you can be honest about seeing yourself and if you can hold to this method. It begins by not expressing negative emotions and then using the pressure this creates to examine the feeling of 'I' behind negative emotions.

It is important to emphasize, however, that not expressing negative emotions does not mean repressing or suppressing them. On the contrary, it means acknowledging them and looking at them as clearly as possible, but doing so without expressing them through any of the four lower centers. You have to contain the energy behind negative emotions if you want to see them for what they are. If their energy slips out, you lose that leverage. This is what non-expression is about.

Containing this energy by not expressing negative emotions has another important side which is to see that the cause of negative emotions is always inside us, not outside. In other words, nothing can cause you to become negative unless you are identified and give yourself permission to be negative about it. This sounds illogical at first, but the more you look behind negative emotions, and the more you see how they are fabricated by the four lower centers, the more you will see that negativity is entirely your responsibility.

Why do you say responsibility?

When you really penetrate the understanding that nothing can make you negative unless you are identified and choose to be negative, you will see that this gives you tremendous freedom. Think about it: you don't have to become negative about anything. You can simply drop this weight if you want to, just as you can be free of identification if you truly want to be free of it. But this freedom comes with an equally big responsibility. Namely, accepting the truth that the cause of negative emotions is in you, in your idea of yourself, in your thinking and attitudes, and that the ego is sustaining itself through negative emotions. It is not that we don't want to give up negative emotions. We do. We just don't want to give up the ego. It doesn't surrender so easily.

You said it does not matter what kind of negative emotion it is because they are all the same thing. What do you mean?

I said the form does not matter. The form of negative emotions varies, but the source behind them and the process of creating them remains the same. Whether you know it or not, when you express negative emotions you are consuming the energy of awareness, chewing it up, and spitting it out. When you realize this, you see that it is sad because it means that awareness was not able to resist identification. It took the bait, was corrupted, and got thrown away.

The root of the word negative means to negate or deny. Negative emotions are 'No' emotions. They say 'No' to reality. In this sense, they are not really emotions. They are negators, resistors, rejectors. They do the opposite of embracing reality. They deny it.

Two examples are irritation and anger. When something is not going our way, we generally resist it with irritation or anger. We use them to deny and reject something. The same is true of depression, which is usually a big 'No' to something. Depression is passive rather than active and it is more subtle than anger, but it is still negativity being expressed through the lower centers. It is still a corruption and leakage of awareness.

Depression feels like a withdrawal into a dark space? How is it a rejection?

It is the ego withdrawing into itself to protect itself from something that it would prefer to avoid or not see. It uses depression as a blindfold and blanket. Deep depression—even sulking—creates an undercurrent of negativity that is hard for awareness to navigate. Awareness has to recognize that it is outside not inside this current, and that the current is really a drawn out manifestation of 'I'. There is a difference between being depressed and seeing your image of self feeling depressed. 'I' am depressed is one thing. Seeing that feeling of 'I' pass through you is something else.

This is another area where it is helpful to know about the four lower centers because virtually all negative emotions originate in the instinctive center and spawn from there. The instinctive center supplies the negative energy that gets transported by identification to the emotional and intellectual centers which convert it into negative emotions.

How do they convert it?

The emotional center adds the personal component, concocts a story and embroiders it, and weaves it into blame or accusation or self-pity. The intellectual center then justifies the feeling of negativity and the rationale for expressing it outwardly. The result is an ego that lets the world know how it feels, be it through visible anger or obstinate withdrawal. Either way it is a form of self-indulgent denial. 'I' get to be angry. 'I' get to feel miserable. And 'I' grows stronger.

It is a beautiful day when you recognize negative emotions as camouflage of the ego. All along you thought you were the feeling of 'I' behind negative emotions, and now you see those feelings are hiding something. Those feelings were never you. And the ego lurking behind those feelings, holding onto them, is not you either. Awareness of all these is the true Self.

I usually know that depression is happening and I don't want it to happen, but it overwhelms me and I sink into it.

The most important thing about what you just said is that you can see it happening. This means that not all of your awareness is sinking into it. And that is your stronghold. As with most negative emotions, depression starts with the instinctive center which then infiltrates the emotional and intellectual centers. Depression can also disable the moving center and prevent you from getting out of bed or off the couch or out of the house. This is because the instinctive center is sitting on top of the other centers.

An image that may help is to envision depression as a rock sitting on top of a beach ball or large balloon. The instinctive weight of the rock pushes down and causes a depression in the emotional balloon. The question then becomes, how to lift the rock off the balloon or how to inflate the balloon so the rock will roll off? What you eat, what you drink, how much you exercise or not, how well you rest at night, and how content or discontent you are with your life all influence the instinctive center. Concerns about health, finances, and relationships also weigh heavily on the instinctive center and can lead to a spiral of negative thoughts and emotions.

Controlling the instinctive center so that the rock is not so heavy can be difficult because the instinctive center manifests mainly through sensations that can be hard for the other centers to interpret. But the more clearly you can pinpoint what is upsetting the instinctive center, the more effectively you can address it. In the case of depression, we usually think it is due to something emotional. We fail to look for its source in the instinctive center, and the rock stays intact.

What is the best way to inflate the balloon?

Inflating the balloon and rolling the rock off do not mean trying to feel artificially happy. That may help for a short time, but we want to go to the source. For example, do 'I' feel resentful about something, guilty about something, or perhaps feel sorry for 'myself' as a victim? Or is it just an opaque feeling of boredom, listlessness, and dullness concealing the real issue beneath. As I mentioned, depression serves as a blanket to cover the cause and to keep the ego comfortable.

If our emotional center was buoyant and healthy, the balloon would be naturally inflated and instinctive rocks would have a hard time settling on top of it. It would take a really big event, a serious shock in your life, to deflate the balloon. But our emotional center is not normally inflated due to all the little negative emotions that are constantly pressing on it. This makes it easy for even small rocks to settle on top and stay there. We have to carry this weight around all the time which makes us susceptible to even more negativity.

The best way to restore the emotional center is by not expressing negative emotions outwardly and not indulging in them internally. This does not mean repressing or suppressing negative emotions. It means looking squarely at them, acknowledging that they exist, and seeing them as reflections of the ego. The method of not expressing a negative emotion is intended to provide leverage so that you can see behind it and underneath it. When you express the negative emotion, you lose this leverage.

You mentioned not being able to get out of bed when you are depressed. Can you talk a little more about that?

If this happens to you, imagine yourself as the rock and your bed as the beach ball. Try not to stay there. Try to get up. Try to make the bed. Straighten the sheets and smooth the cover and envision the same thing happening to your emotional center.

Same thing if you are on the couch in a low mood. Try to get up, tidy the couch, fluff up the pillows. If you can, get out of the house and go for a walk. Purposely fill your mind with impressions of the city and nature. Call someone. Talk to someone. Beauty, friendship, and nature nourish the emotional center and restore it to normal health.

This is also where it gets interesting because you will notice that the instinctive center does not want the emotional center to feel better. It wants you to stay in bed, on the couch, isolated in the house. Behind this inertia is the sense of 'me' burrowed in the ego. The same thing is true when you are angry. The instinctive center does not want the emotional center to calm down. Behind your aggression you will see that your sense of 'I' refuses to budge.

Neither depression nor anger is easy to get out of. They both demonstrate how hard it is to transform negative emotions even when you know about this idea and want to do it. The physical and psychological inertia in both cases is very strong. For a long time all you can do is ride them out, knowing that you are riding them out. But a day will come when a small crack appears in the ego's armor and you glimpse the truth behind the anger or depression. The light of awareness enters their darkness and sees your imaginary self suffering and wanting to suffer through the anger or depression. But because the light of awareness has entered, the negative emotion can never claim a complete hold over you again. Even if it tries and succeeds for a time, it can never operate entirely in the dark again. The absence of awareness was its greatest advantage and now the light starts to have the advantage.

What about medication for depression and for anger? Isn't it sometimes necessary?

It may be necessary depending on the individual. When there are serious underlying medical conditions they should certainly be addressed by a doctor. What I was describing applies to relatively healthy people whose problems stem largely from negative emotions and who are interested in breaking through to a higher dimension of awareness. The techniques I mentioned can work for anyone and make them feel better for awhile, but you can never break completely free from negative emotions as long as the ego stays intact behind them.

Psychotherapy can also help.

In the case of self-realization, it can help only up to a point because psychotherapy is a tool invented by the mind to work on the mind for the mind's sake. It does not take into account how a lapse of awareness leads to identification. Psychotherapy studies the results of identification and regards that as the problem without seeing that the problem is identification itself. Psychotherapy also never pieces together the connections between awareness, identification, the lower centers, the ego, and negative emotions. It focuses primarily on the ego without recognizing awareness as a different dimension of consciousness.

Are you recommending against psychotherapy?

I am just pointing out its limitations with respect to the self-realization of awareness. For example, psychotherapy is designed to help Peter come to terms with his depressive mood without realizing that it is addressing his ego, not awareness. What I am saying is that it is not a matter of Peter learning how to get out of depression, but a matter of awareness releasing its identification with Peter; that this is the deeper cause of the depression. The cause was never an event or person or ailment as much as it was Peter's imaginary idea of himself as a person who needs and wants and thinks he deserves to have certain things or to be treated a certain way by others.

Psychotherapy can be very useful in helping you see this side of yourself. But the purpose should not be to dig and dig and dig into the ego. That just reinforces the ego. Nor should the purpose be to dull the ego with drugs. The purpose should be to expose the ego and open the gate for awareness to liberate itself from the ego. In right order you discover that awareness was never depressed. It was simply identified with the ego's needs and wants and fears.

Think how huge this is, especially considering how many people live with depression, take strong medication for depression, and think there is no alternative. And these numbers are growing as the idea of mental illness becomes more popular and more socially acceptable. It is almost an epidemic. Meanwhile, awareness is stuck and cannot get out because it does not realize that it can get out. It is identified and thinks it is the ego.

Are there any other ways to fend off depression or deal with it as it is happening?

Another way is housecleaning. It sounds too simple, but the value of doing housework and making things cleaner is that it has a positive effect on all four of the lower centers. To do housework, you have to be moving. The moving center in turn impacts the instinctive center by promoting blood circulation, healthy breathing, use of the muscles, and so on. As you concentrate on cleaning, attention is taken away from the intellectual center which can no longer wallow in a mire of negative thoughts. And as things get cleaner, their bright appearance lifts the emotional center. Beauty, even simple beauty, inflates the balloon. The effort to tidy up also makes you feel good because you are accomplishing something visible. Meher Baba said that "the observance of external cleanliness brightens to an extent the internal life." He was referring to this method. When you do it consciously, it is extremely useful. Even if you are not angry or depressed, cleaning your home can lift your spirits, which really means bring awareness back into focus.

You can experience the same thing by taking a walk and noticing everything around you. At first it may be hard to break through the cloud of thoughts associated with a bad mood, but slowly those will clear, especially when you are consciously taking a walk for this reason. You will start seeing the world in front of you. The sense of 'I' will diminish. Awareness will rise out of the four centers and know itself as pure perception looking through your eyes.

That sounds easy, but I know how hard it can be to shake off a heavy mood even when I want to. Why do you think it is so hard?

I agree. It is hard. Or perhaps it is more accurate to say that it is slow, especially when you are first learning to dissolve identification. We have established many years of psychological inertia. The feeling of 'me' is so deeply entrenched that it feels right to be in a heavy mood. We also have little experience with the alternative of consciously popping out of it and leaving 'me' behind.

When intense sensations, thoughts, and feelings arise, they leave their footprints in the mind. The heavier they are and the more we identify with them, the deeper their footprint. Later, when a situation evokes that part of the mind where a footprint is, the footprint beckons the original thoughts and emotions to come fill it up again. There are many footprints like this that get petrified in our psyche.

Think of your own mind and all the footprints left there, like a sandy road where thousands of people have walked and where some pathways are deeper worn than others. Those are our habitual ways of thinking and feeling.

Normal psychology might tell you to get a shovel and fill each footprint with sand to prevent what I just described from repeating itself. But that would take forever and it might not work. A faster way would be to rake the road with a special tool that could rake the entire road smooth at once, in an instant. This tool is awareness.

When you understand that all negative emotions, all moods, all resentments, and so on are essentially the same phenomenon at work, you can rake them all clean. Raking one rakes them all and the mind is immediately smooth again. But you have to do this consciously, knowing that it goes against all the impulses of the ego.

What do you mean that all negative emotions are the same phenomenon?

They are all manifestations of the same ego. They look different, but it is the same ego wearing different shoes. It likes to leave its imprints in the mind so it can retrace those steps again and again. Some eastern traditions refer to the egoic mind as one large bundle of thoughts. Once you see them as part of the same bundle it is easier to toss them all out at the same time. When one of them appears, you toss out the whole bundle. You keep returning to an empty mind and starting again as pure presence.

Intense suffering can also disperse thoughts and rake the mind clean of most traces of the ego, sometimes temporarily and sometimes permanently.

What about death?

Death reveals the ego as an illusion. It demolishes that illusion. The question is whether awareness is conscious enough at that point to watch the illusion vanish and not be affected, not vanish along with it.

Do you consider anxiety a form of depression?

Anxiety may lead to depression, but they are not the same. For instance, feeling anxious is one thing, which stems from the instinctive center. Becoming anxious about feeling anxious is another thing, which stems from the emotional center. Seeing both is another. And being aware that you are seeing them is yet another. These are four different dimensions of being.

You can look at depression the same way. You start to feel depressed, then you add a layer and feel depressed about being depressed. The question is whether these two layers completely absorb awareness or whether you can distinguish between them and rise above them as awareness.

Is it really possible to stop a negative emotion?

The truth is that you cannot stop it until you know how to stop identification. A negative emotion is a psychological entity formed by identification out of the material of unconscious awareness. When awareness is not conscious of itself as awareness, it becomes identification. As you examine negative emotions in yourself, you will see that awareness and identification are different aspects of the same thing. They transform into each other. One is conscious. The other is not.

The process of unconscious awareness transforming into identification is, ironically, due to awareness looking for itself, but doing so through psychological and physical form rather than as metaphysical awareness. When we are identified, we are looking in the wrong direction for identity. The mystery of existence is that life as a human being can become an opportunity for awareness to reverse this tendency, find its way out of identification, and return to itself as conscious awareness. Transforming negative emotions and transforming suffering are directly tied to this possibility.

I notice that most of my anxiety is about the future in general. There doesn't seem to be a specific worry.

You have to see that something in you wants this general anxiety. More specifically, the ego wants it, allows it, and indulges it. Look closely and you will also see that anxiety about the future originates as uneasiness in the instinctive center. This sense of uneasiness then prompts negative feelings in the emotional center and produces negative thoughts in the intellectual center. It becomes a spiral that unwinds as a weave of me, my problems, and my worries, which leads to psychological tension and often physical illness. As awareness begins to recognize itself outside this conglomeration, the knot of 'me' starts to loosen, the sense of 'I' starts to dissolve, and the spiral stops turning. You find yourself floating in the void of awareness, going nowhere, anticipating nothing, comprehending everything.

In terms of anxiety, we can think about the past and future, but we don't need to. We can worry about tomorrow, but we don't need to. Behind all the things we don't need, what remains? Only awareness. You have to prefer this void of presence. But it is not even a matter of preferring it. As awareness expands, anxiety dissolves because there is no longer any material or room for it. It gets absorbed by awareness.

(pause)

Our real anxiety is that deep down we want to return to the source of awareness. At some point we realize this and start looking for a way out. What we don't realize at first, however, is that we the person cannot get out. Only awareness gets out.

Are we not also identified with the desire to return to the source of awareness?

Yes, but that comes later, and then you realize what I just said: that only awareness escapes. What you are describing is a deeper layer of the ego that is still holding on in the name of 'me' desiring self-realization.

Earlier when you were talking about negative emotions you said awareness can learn to return to itself. How does it do this?

Awareness has a peculiar quality that is timeless. It can find itself identified and in that exact instant bring itself home as conscious awareness. This is because there is no time element or space element in awareness. The same thing is true about identification, which is the flip side of awareness. Both of them always exist in the now, never in the past or future. And when they transform into each other, they do so now.

This special quality of awareness is hinted at in the story of the prodigal son who returned to his father's home simply by wanting to be there. It is also how Dorothy in "The Wizard of Oz" got back to Kansas. She was even told that she had always possessed this capability. She just didn't know it. The same is true of awareness. It doesn't realize itself. But as soon as it does, it is home again.

You can also think of identification and self-realization as different charges in the flow of awareness. Identification is a downward flow from positive to negative. Self-realization is an upward flow from negative to positive. When you stop identifying, the charge switches from negative to positive and the energy of awareness flows up. This is the essence of the idea of transforming negative emotions into positive emotions by learning not to identify.

Does a negative emotion itself become a positive emotion? Can you give an example of that?

The mind wants to understand this idea as a logical exchange, but it is more than that. For instance, anger does not turn into love. Depression does not become happiness. If they did, it would imply that your sense of 'I'—the ego—is feeling one way and then feels another way that is better.

When you first encounter the idea of transformation, it seems reasonable to assume that you can transform negative emotions by means of acceptance and letting go; that you will be able to shake off the negativity and feel differently. But then you discover it is not as simple as that because it is not a matter of shaking off a negative emotion. It is a matter of dissolving the 'I' that is experiencing the negative emotion. Only when that dissolves can transformation happen. This is because transformation does not happen to 'I'. It happens to awareness. When you understand this, you stop trying to shake off the negative emotion. You focus instead on releasing identification with the sense of 'I' behind it which feels 'I' am angry or 'I' am depressed or 'I' am worried.

The same thing applies to resistance. When you first learn about giving up resistance, it is 'I' that tries to let go and give up its resistance to something. You as awareness have to let go of 'I' first. The resistance will then fall away by itself.

This also ties back to what I mentioned earlier about all negative emotions being the same phenomenon. Whatever we are identified with, and whatever type of negative emotion forms in response to it, those are not the main point. The main point is the 'I' that has wrapped the negative emotion around itself. It wears all negative emotions like different cloaks and takes on the flavor of each one, but behind all of them you find this imaginary sense of 'I' and 'me'.

When it comes to transformation, we are not talking about transforming the cloak of a negative emotion. We are talking about the feeling of 'I' behind it, and about awareness being transformed by seeing 'I' as an impostor. When awareness sees this, 'I' goes limp, the cloak of negativity falls off, and awareness rises. The energy that was bolstering 'I' gets released and lifts awareness, which is a liberating experience because it reverses what had been a negative charge into a positive flow of conscious energy.

So it is not so much a matter of trying to resolve the negative emotion itself?

To expose 'I', you may still need to work your way through the cloak, through the psychological justification that the ego is using to cling to the negativity. At a certain point, however, when you experience a negative emotion, you learn to look right at the feeling of 'I' behind it. As awareness transcends that feeling, the negative emotion will transform. Deprived of its nucleus of identification, it will change form, dissolve into pure energy, and release that energy to awareness.

When the energy behind a negative emotion is released to awareness, it becomes a booster rocket that propels awareness from the surface of the mind and into its own orbit. Harnessing that energy begins with the non-expression of negative emotions. When you withhold the expression of a negative emotion, you contain the energy behind it. You cocoon the ego so that its constituent parts can dissolve and be reconstituted as energy for awareness. But for this to work, awareness has to contain itself and see what is going on. Transformation always begins and ends with awareness.

I still don't quite understand how the feeling of 'I' transforms into awareness.

The feeling of 'I' itself does not transform into awareness. It is better to say that the energy of identification behind 'I' gets transformed. As awareness transcends the sense of 'I' behind negative emotions, the energy that had been spent on resisting things like discomfort, inconvenience, pain, and suffering gets released to awareness. This energy passes from the dimension of 'I' to the dimension of awareness. In the process it changes form. That is what transformation means. It means crossing over to, or into, a higher dimension. Suddenly, awareness is there just behind you, quietly and imperceptibly aware of being aware.

Is this the Phoenix rising from the ashes?.

Yes. The Phoenix of awareness is rising from the ashes of negative emotions which were the result of identification. What often gets missed in that image, however, is that it works both ways. The Phoenix also falls into identification and burns up in the form of negative emotions. When it remembers that it is the Phoenix, it rises. The same idea is expressed slightly differently in The Lord's Prayer which says, in effect, lead us not into the temptation of identification, and deliver us from the evil of negative emotions. The prayer is the mind appealing to awareness not to lose itself in the ashes.

Is that true of all prayers?

It is true of the original meaning behind prayer. If you think in terms of mind, body, and awareness, prayer is about the body yielding, the mind appealing, and awareness realizing. This is why people originally got on their knees to pray. It represented the body kneeling in deference to awareness. Clasping the hands represented the mind containing itself, acknowledging awareness as a higher dimension than itself, and appealing to that dimension for sustenance and support. The Lord's Prayer begins with 'Our father which art in heaven" and ends with 'For thine is the kingdom and the power and the glory'. In other words, it starts with and ends with awareness. It is all about awareness.

Seeing prayer this way turns religion inside-out because you realize that religions are usually understood in terms of us as people rather than us as awareness. Religions focus on the nature of our thoughts and the behavior of our body under the watchful eye of a three-dimensional parent figure in the clouds. They lose sight of awareness and replace it with a concept of god.

The problem of god is not new. How do you understand god?

The problem has never been with god. It has always been with the word and the concept and the interpretation of both. When you peel away the word and look beyond the concept, you find yourself staring into a void of unknowing. The same thing happens when you peel away your name and look beyond the concept of yourself as a person. You are left with the void of awareness, which is the same void beyond the concept of god. It is all one void. But this does not compute mentally because the mind needs concepts and labels and logical explanations. It can't envision nothing. It has to place everything in a relatable context, which is what it does with the idea of prayer and god.

The Lord's Prayer also talks about forgiveness. How is that connected to awareness?

The original version of that prayer talked about forgiving debts. Later it became sins and trespasses. From there it took on the meaning of being pardoned for our transgressions and doing the same for other people. But when you transfer this idea from the world of people to the world of thoughts and awareness, it looks very different, especially when you examine the meaning of debt and the word forgive.

For instance, one way to think about it is that forgive means to fore-give; that is, to give in advance. In this case, to give in advance something which is due, such as a birthright. With The Lord's Prayer it can be interpreted as the mind asking the source of awareness to give us in advance our birthright of awareness, just as we will honor the same birthright in others before anything else in them, and before they ask us to.

Suppose, for instance, upon meeting people the first thing you do is acknowledge the awareness in them. Not by telling them that, but by remembering it and being aware of it while you are with them, and regardless of whether or not they are aware of their own awareness or yours. This is the deeper meaning of 'Do unto others as you would have them do unto you'. That is, acknowledge the awareness in others as you would have them acknowledge the same in you. It has nothing to do with kindnesses and gifts and retribution, just as forgiveness is not about pardoning actions or behavior after the fact. For awareness, there is no need for that anyway because awareness just sees people acting according to their degree of awareness in the present moment without any reference to the past or future. The mind judges people and then thinks it needs to forgive them. Awareness resides outside that mental loop.

But you can't expect the world to operate that way. People break laws and do terrible things. We can't just see them as they are and move on.

No, we can't. But now we are talking on the level of the mind and body. On that level and in that dimension, yes, we need laws and prisons because not enough people are consciously aware. They have a low degree of consciousness and conscience, so they cannot regulate themselves from the perspective of awareness. At the same time, awareness never punishes anyone or puts anyone in prison.

It is also the case that no one commits a crime because they think it is wrong or bad. They do it because they think it is right and that it will do them good in some way. At a certain level of identification, that is how it seems and people act accordingly.

This is described very well in Dostoevsky's novel, *Crime and Punishment.* His main character commits murder because he wants to see if he can do it without feeling guilty about it. He also thinks his victim deserves it and that her death will not matter in the larger scheme of things. It never occurs to him that it is wrong or bad. He sees it as a challenge.

Jesus also said, "Forgive them, for they know not what they do."

He was fore-giving in the sense of acknowledging their degree of awareness and accepting the suffering it caused him. It was not a pardon. It was a conscious recognition of reality which enabled him to transform it.

When you examine the idea of forgiveness from the perspective of awareness, you see there is nothing substantial about 'I' forgive 'you' or 'you' forgive 'me'. They are mental constructs of identity in the ego. Being the sinner and being the forgiver are both ego images based on identification. One image feels good. The other feels bad. Take identification away and it looks very different.

Few people are consciously controlling what they do. The instinctive center and ego are controlling them. That is what Jesus saw, which is more obvious when you read the story as an instruction, not as a real event. Whoever wrote that story was trying to instruct us about awareness.

Are you inferring that awareness does not judge other people no matter what they do?

Yes. Judgment never forms as a perception in awareness. That happens only in the mind which responds to everything in terms of right or wrong, black or white, good or bad. To the mind, if something is not one, it has to be the other. This is how the legal system, the educational system, and the parental system all work. These systems enable the mind to function with little or no awareness in what seems to it an orderly way. The mind brings this same form of narrow thinking to all negative emotions, not just to judgment.

Little forms of judgment seem almost ongoing throughout my day. I judge other people, myself, my job, the government. But it feels as though I just have a critical mind.

This is a good observation. Everyone is prone to judging and it takes many forms. For example, we nitpick, criticize, complain, disapprove, accuse, blame, and gossip. We are equally prone to self-judgment which turns into self-deprecation, self-pity, guilt, and depression which are all different manifestations of the ego. When you examine each of them, you see that they are negating and resisting something. When you understand how judgment works in you like this, it will help you see the same thing about other negative emotions.

Judgment is particularly interesting because no one is free of it and everyone thinks it feels right. Although each of us has a proclivity for certain negative emotions, we all tend toward judgment. We carry our own psychological brand of measuring stick for evaluating other people, events, and the world in general. When someone or something measures up to our standards, we judge them positively. Otherwise we judge them negatively. It is alarming to see the flavor of your own built-in capacity for judging and to realize how feeble it is.

Something to notice about judgment is that it starts with irritation, usually as irritation in the instinctive center. But it flashes so quickly from there and into the emotional center that it feels like it came from the emotional center. You have to be alert to see that it originates in the instinctive center and spawns from there. This also shows the close link between the instinctive center and the ego. They usually get annoyed together and resist together. We end up perceiving through their lens and reacting from them rather than seeing and accepting things as they are. It is not easy to look past the veil of judgment. You have to see it as a veil and slip through it. On the other side of it there is a huge vista that judgment deprives us of.

What did Jesus mean that judgment is the beam in our eye?

It is noteworthy that he called it a beam. He did not say we had to remove the splinter in our eye before we removed the splinter in the other person. For one thing, a wooden beam is made up of a whole bunch of splinters. The entire collection of our own faults. For another, a beam can be a shaft, in this case the psychological shaft of our tendency to judge. Jesus may have been implying that the inherent tendency to judge is much larger than any fault we might find in somebody else. A beam can also mean a reflection of light that shines in your face and blocks your view, which is what judgment does.

The idea of a beam also suggests an obstacle that stands in our way. This is what judgment does. It is a psychological stopping point. We see something, interpret it a certain way, and then stop at the conclusion of our interpretation. We do the same thing with all negative emotions. We stop and think, 'that's it, that's how it is'. But there's more beyond it if we can remove the obstacle in ourselves that is preventing us from seeing further. Beyond any negative emotion there is a clear view of things as they are. So when you find yourself judging other people, yourself, or circumstances, think about trying to go further. Think about jumping over that beam or passing through it as pure awareness. Keep looking with awareness.

I have heard you say that the mind itself cannot see. What do you mean?

The mind is an organ that registers information, analyzes ideas, compares things, and draws logical conclusions. Most of the information it accumulates comes in through the eyes and ears and is immediately filtered into mental images and concepts. The mind then disconnects from vision and hearing to revolve in its own thoughts. At that point you are no longer looking or listening. You are immersed in the thought world and only vaguely see or hear what is going on around you. The mind is seeing and hearing only its thoughts. And, in truth, it never was perceiving the world directly. It was relying entirely on the eyes and ears to do that on its behalf.

The eyes and ears, as well as the nose and mouth, are an interesting study. They are each a portal for the five senses and to varying degrees they are all in close proximity to the brain. But the eyes are the most remarkable due to their direct connection to the brain via the orbital nerve which makes the eyes almost an external part of the brain. The eyes put the brain directly in touch with light and the many reflections of light that we depend on for so many things.

Another interesting thing about the eyes is that they also do not see. This sounds strange at first, but when you notice how vision works, you see that the eyes are simply instruments for the lower centers to see with, and for awareness to see through. The instinctive center uses these instruments much of the time to meet its constant needs. The other centers use them as necessary, for instance when the moving center handles an object, or the intellectual center reads, or the emotional center admires a flower arrangement. Awareness perceives all of these, but instead of seeing *with* the eyes as they do, it sees *through* the eyes, as William Blake said.

What are we seeing when we look at the eyes of human beings?

The eyes of human beings are not easy to read because there are four centers connected to them. You cannot always be sure which center you are looking at. The best thing is to learn to recognize which center in you is using your own eyes in a given moment. For instance, the instinctive center looks with an intense energy that can be sharp, acquisitive, aggressive, suspicious, or manipulative. The moving center has a relatively neutral gaze that registers objects in space and how objects move and connect in space. The intellectual center has a linear gaze that is in search of labels and information and definitions. The emotional center has a gaze that is welcoming, appreciative, yearning, joyful, expectant, pleading, sorrowful, empathetic. Being able to recognize all these nuances in your own gaze can be useful.

When you look at another person, you may notice that their gaze is clouded because they are preoccupied with their thought world and barely looking out of their eyes. Other times they may be looking out, but behind their eyes there is something fearful and guarded, so they maintain a forceful gaze that does not let other people in. Many things about our inner character as well as our degree of awareness are visible in the eyes.

Most of the time, however, people do not look into each other's eyes this way. They look at each other, but not into each other. The instinctive center also does not like to be seen, so our instinctive centers establish a silent agreement not to stare at one another. We even go so far as to consider it impolite. But when you do look with more awareness, you see that everything happening in the face is a reflection of what is happening behind the eyes. In this respect, the eyes are the gateway to the soul as well as to the four lower centers.

Is our vision different when conscious awareness looks through the eyes?

When awareness is more conscious, it looks through the eyes with transparency and clarity. The eyes may also reflect how awareness is perceiving the outer world while simultaneously glimpsing inner worlds, as though occupying both dimensions at the same time. The nineteenth-century naturalist John Burroughs, who was a friend of Walt Whitman, wrote in his journal that one day when Walt turned and looked at him, "It was as though the earth turned and looked at me."

Why does the instinctive center weigh so heavily on the emotional center? I am thinking about your example of the rock and the balloon with depression.

The instinctive center governs the physiology of our whole body including the operation of the five senses. Together, the five senses inform the moving center, the intellectual center, and the emotional center. So the instinctive center is really the brain behind the other three centers and behind our entire organism, which makes it very powerful. In this sense it dominates the other centers and can manipulate them behind the scenes. At the same time, it is not easily discernible to the other three centers so it can convince itself and them that it is awareness.

As you hear me saying this, you might notice a heightened energy mounting inside you, filling your body and head. That is the instinctive center reacting to being talked about. Most people aren't aware of the instinctive center, but as you do become aware of it the instinctive center will deflect attention from itself so as not to be perceived. It is so good at this that awareness often notices the instinctive center only in the rear view mirror, after the fact; after the instinctive center has prompted a decision or action in one of the other centers.

I would like to hear more about negative emotions starting in the instinctive center and spreading from there to the other centers.

The instinctive center is also the source of subliminal sensations that become material for anxieties, worries, fears, notions of revenge, morose ideas, imaginary scenarios, pessimism, and perverse thoughts, to name just a few. These sensations become emotional only when the emotional center picks them up and churns them. The important thing to know is that they originate as sensations, not as feelings in the emotional center, although that is how we usually interpret them.

It is not uncommon for these kind of sensations to surge in the middle of the night when the instinctive center holds full sway over the moving, intellectual, and emotional centers and can infiltrate them with whatever it wants to. The same sensations occur during the day when we encounter inconveniences like traffic delays, interruptions, obstacles to our projects, tension with other people, and many other examples.

What happens is that the emotional center picks up this energy, blends it with its own energy, and turns the mix into feelings of irritation, accusation, blame, anger, self-pity, guilt, worry, moodiness, resentment, depression, and so on. The intellectual center then corroborates by providing rationale for the way the emotional center is beginning to feel. What started as a sensation in the gut turns into an embroidered story of problems and woes. The moving center then joins in to demonstrate and display those woes. The eventual expression of negativity is an elimination of this corrupt mix of energy that was manufactured and passed through all the centers. Trace it back and you will see that it all started in the instinctive center.

Since they start in the instinctive center, why are they called emotions?

Because they become emotions with the help of the emotional center. The instinctive center simply provides the negative energy. Specifically, it is energy generated by the negative half of the instinctive center and then turned into negative emotions by the negative half of the emotional center. It may take a long time to realize that what feel like valid emotions have their origin in the instinctive center, and that they become negative only because you identify with them and indulge them. If you hold to the concept of how negative emotions are manufactured, you will see that the urge to become negative has its roots in the instinctive center. You will see that negative emotions are like ligaments the ego depends on for support. Without them it falls apart the same way a scarecrow falls apart when it loses its straw.

From what you said it sounds like the instinctive center would not be too happy about this. Does that change as awareness grows?

Awareness does not displace the instinctive center. It simply casts more and more light on it. At the same time, seeing the instinctive center as it really is can be discomfiting. It is like peeling off your skin and seeing what is underneath. When you really see it, you see the extent to which it governs your predilection for indulging in negative emotions and expressing them. When you see yourself or someone else expressing negative emotions, look behind the expression and you will see the instinctive center. When you encounter stiff resistance in yourself or in another person, you are also face-to-face with it. You simply cannot reason with the instinctive center in yourself or in another person. You have to find another way.

And you are right. The instinctive center is not happy about being seen and having its association with the ego exposed. When this happens it may respond with different subterfuges. Among these are all sorts of physical sensations, pains, and ailments as well as extreme, bizarre, or vainglorious thoughts. This is what Jesus being tempted by the devil is about. The Christ consciousness within him was being challenged by the ego at its root in the instinctive center.

Is the devil also an example of the instinctive center feigning awareness?

It is more an example of the instinctive center trying to reclaim its territory as number one. When I mentioned feigning, I was referring to how the instinctive center radiates with a magnetism of alertness that is impressive to the mind and body; so impressive that that they think it is awareness, which it is in a physical sense. But this alertness is the same you find in animals, whereas conscious awareness is not energy or magnetism. It is a field of formless consciousness that perceives energy, including the energy of the instinctive center. This is baffling to the instinctive center because it knows nothing higher than itself. At the same time, it senses the presence of awareness, feels threatened by it, and furtively recoils so as not to be seen by it. If the instinctive center cannot supplant awareness, it slinks away. But it inevitably returns to wage another war.

You also have to remember that the instinctive center is designed to protect itself and survive. It is not deliberately trying to undermine awareness. It does not even comprehend the nature of awareness. It just knows that it is under threat by something so it raises its hackles, fires it darts, and tries to camouflage itself. It is not bad. It simply cannot react any differently. At the same time, it wants you to identify with it, take it seriously, be afraid of it, feel sorry for it, get upset with it, complain about it, fight back. Anything that keeps awareness preoccupied with the four lower centers keeps the instinctive center feeling in charge, and this is what the devil represents. He was essentially saying to awareness, "I will give you whatever you want in terms of the body and mind as long as I get to be in charge."

You said that negative emotions are resistors and rejectors. Why do we feel the need to resist and reject so much?

As human beings we naturally resist anything that disturbs our comfort. Our comfort is mainly instinctive, but it can also be emotional and intellectual. Whenever any of the centers encounters an obstacle to its momentum or an interruption to its comfort, there is tension and pressure. The fourth way calls it friction to imply that when things rub against each other they generate a charge of energy which we experience as tension and pressure. The tendency of the lower centers and the instinctive center in particular is to avoid, resist, and complain about tension and pressure.

The energy produced by friction is a form of heat. When pressure builds in the mind and body, it creates heat and the lower centers recoil from it. The more they recoil, the more our sense of 'I' solidifies in the lower centers. Resistance to friction is one of the pillars of the ego in terms of how it forms. When we resist, we solidify our sense of 'I'.

But it can happen another way. Instead of identifying with pressure and suffering, awareness can transform the heat of friction by becoming conscious of itself watching the mind and body as they endure pressure and suffering. In other words, awareness can use friction as a catalyst to distill the heat into greater awareness. The heat of friction can evaporate as conscious awareness.

Friction is like the heat on the stove. Our lower centers feeling pressure and pain are the water in the pot. The molecules of awareness are inherent in the water vapor that is released into the air. However, when it comes to pressure in our lives, we prefer to turn off the heat or remove the pot from the stove.

In this analogy, the ego is like a lid on the pot. It makes it harder for molecules of awareness to escape into the air. Without this lid, the heat of friction would boil the water of mind and body and enable the molecules of awareness to rise and escape.

You might think this is what happens when

we express negative emotions, but it is not the case because awareness does not evaporate as itself when we express negative emotions. Instead, we reach a boiling point, the lid pops off, and the molecules of awareness simply splash out as volatile negativity instead of rising as consciousness awareness. This is the norm. For it to happen differently, you have to understand the components and the whole process, and awareness has to be conscious of itself.

In physics, the greater the pressure and the more dense the liquid, the more heat is required to achieve evaporation. Less density and less pressure equal easier, faster evaporation. The same is true in the realm of body, mind, ego, and awareness. The less dense our psychology is and the lighter the ego is, the easier and faster awareness can consciously transform itself.

Does more awareness make the pain and suffering go away?

It makes the identification go away, which releases the energy from pain and suffering. They remain, but they are less charged because your identity is less wrapped up in them. From the perspective of awareness, pain and suffering are not bad things. On the contrary: without them awareness cannot distill itself. But you cannot think seriously about transforming them until you can transcend negative emotions. Otherwise you stay stuck in the negative emotions that are resisting them. When that barrier is removed you can fully accept the suffering and use it to elevate awareness.

True suffering, as Peter Ouspensky said, is a kind of fermentation. Among other things, he was suggesting that it has chemical properties which under the right circumstances can neutralize identification and disable the ego for a shorter or longer time, or permanently. This is significant because the ego is our major block to awareness. Suffering can act as a solvent that dissolves the ego and clears a channel for awareness to flow freely as itself. Yielding to the force of suffering can be transformative because it makes the energy behind suffering available to awareness. I mentioned before that there is energy behind negative emotions. There is even more energy behind deep suffering. Identification converts this energy into negative emotions whereas non-identification transforms it into awareness.

But it is important to understand that the energy behind negative emotions and the energy of suffering are tapped in different ways.

When negative emotions appear, you contain their outer expression. This creates an internal pressure that wedges open the space between awareness and the feeling of 'I' so awareness can realize itself. When suffering comes it is different because you don't have to contain it. Rather, you have to open yourself to it so its force of energy can flow through you without resistance. When you do this consciously, the force of suffering transmutes the energy behind your feeling of 'I' into a deeper self-realization of awareness.

Both are very powerful because they mean transitioning from the dimension of 'I am negative' and 'I am suffering' to the dimension of pure awareness being conscious of itself. We normally experience negative emotions and suffering as aspects of our identity. Through conscious transformation they become catalysts for awareness.

Does death provide the best opportunity for transforming suffering?

I would say it depends on the consciousness of the person and how they die. Awareness cannot transcend the body until it transcends suffering. It cannot transcend suffering until it transcends negative emotions. And it cannot transcend negative emotions until it transcends the sense of 'I' and ego. Walt Whitman wrote, "Rise after rise bow the phantoms behind me."

I notice that we resist and reject in different ways. My husband, for example, gets upset and negative about pressure differently than I do.

Yes, it is not the same for everyone. Each person has a predominant psychological tendency referred to in the fourth way as 'chief weakness' or 'chief feature'. This tendency lies at the core of our sense of 'I'. It lends the main color to the ego's palette and it infiltrates all our perceptions, reactions, decisions, and justifications. The core of chief feature is hard to pinpoint because it radiates through our entire physiology and psychology. But its roots can be detected in the kind of negative emotions it produces and the logic it uses to justify them.

In this sense, negative emotions are the weak spot of chief feature. There are always certain negative emotions that chief feature cannot resist. For instance, some people are prone to anger, some to self-pity, some to resentment, some to indignation, some to fear. Each person has a proclivity when it comes to negative emotions and their chief feature exercises this proclivity when expressing negative emotions. With some people chief feature explodes. With others it implodes. And with others it simmers. It each case, the expression of negative emotions is the most full-blown manifestation of their ego and one of the most visible signs of chief feature.

I also notice that if one of us is negative we want the other to be negative, too.

This is strange, isn't it? We not only throw negative emotions at each other to hurt each other, we try to slip negativity into each other's pockets to get it off our back and onto someone else's. We don't want the weight. We want somebody else to carry it. And couples often trade negativity back and forth. Now that you're negative, I don't have to be, at least not until you find a way to give it back to me. This also happens in couples because together they become an intertwined instinctive center. The game of tossing negativity back and forth progresses swiftly and antagonistically.

The best thing in this case is for one person not to catch the negativity when it gets thrown at them. Or not to pick it up when it is put in their pocket or placed at their feet. Even then it is tempting to show that you are purposely not picking it up, which is still a subtle way of expressing negativity. In the end it comes down to not being identified with the other person's negativity, and not being identified with the fact that you are negative about them being negative.

When both people understand what is really happening, it is helpful to have a hug. A physical hug can break the negative charge between two instinctive centers and loosen the identification all around. Often without knowing it, this is why couples have make-up sex, although that is not the best way to neutralize negativity. The best way is to see through the negativity and transform it with conscious awareness. That is what makes a bond truly stronger and more mature.

Is chief feature visible under normal circumstances when we are not upset or negative?

Yes. Chief feature governs our actions and

reactions in many ways. One way is in how you respond to different situations. Do you charge ahead, try to take control, back off, hesitate, resist, withdraw? Each chief feature fosters the notion that it can impose itself onto situations and steer events actively or passively or indifferently, depending on the feature.

The ego wraps itself around chief feature, takes on its characteristics, and projects them into the world as behavior. The moment we open our mouths or start to act, the ego transports itself through the mind and body, and the character of our behavior changes according to the kind of chief feature we have. It is hard not to project this image of ourselves, just as it is hard not to endorse the image which other people project of themselves. It shows you the power that chief feature has over us.

When you start to see this it becomes uncomfortable. You realize how much this force in you is driving your behavior. You also realize that it is not you, not awareness. Most people are oblivious to their feature. They are either comfortable in it or suffering because of it, but in neither case do they understand the extent to which they are governed by it. It is difficult to see that chief feature is our weak point precisely because it is our weak point. To see it, we have to be outside it as awareness.

Although chief feature is behind our perceptions, decisions, and actions, a general exception to this is when we are alone, calm, and not thinking about other people and how they perceive us. The ego is not needed then, so chief feature settles down and we can be our simple selves. The fourth way refers to this as essence. Our essence stands in striking contrast to the artificial personality that gets projected by chief feature and the ego. Essence is unassuming, unpretentious, genuine, delicate. It is also the natural well spring of awareness. All it has to do is realize that its own simple presence is the foundation of awareness.

The opposite extreme of essence is when chief feature surges and displaces essence with identification and negative emotions. This is what Eckhart Tolle calls the pain body. It is the mental-emotional 'body' of the ego reassembling itself with the psychological arguments and armor of chief feature.

Is our personality the mask of the ego?

Yes, although personality is more than a mask. It is also a curtain that shuts awareness in and distorts what it perceives. The ego hides behind the curtain and holds awareness prisoner as it projects its image to the world.

How is essence the well spring of awareness?

Essence is awareness in innocent form. It is innocent because it is not aware of itself as awareness. You see this in small children when unadulterated awareness is looking through their eyes without any consciousness of itself as awareness. It is one reason we adore newborns and small children. We recognize the purity of their awareness as something familiar. It is also no accident that when awareness realizes itself there is a feeling of being newly born.

You said that friction causes tension. I feel the tension but I usually can't get rid of it. Is there something specific I can do?

We always want to do something about it. We want to change ourselves or change others or change circumstances. We want them to change in accordance with our preferences. In other words, we want to apply pressure back on the pressure so it will change. But this never works because two active forces meeting each other and butting heads only creates more tension.

The truth is that change happens by itself under the influence of awareness. Perhaps a better way to say it is that the light of awareness influences change. For instance, as you become aware of physical tension and sustain that awareness without trying to do anything to the tension, the body starts to relax. Similarly, as you become aware of thoughts and just see them without trying to stop them, the mind starts to quieten. And as you become aware of perceiving, awareness starts to be aware of itself. This is because the body is inherently still, the mind inherently quiet, and awareness inherently conscious. The true nature of each already exists and just has to be realized.

When they are realized, the structure of the body returns to stillness, without tension. The framework of the mind becomes a quiet backdrop, absent of compulsion. Awareness rediscovers consciousness without identification. The combination of all these is bliss.

Is this achieved by letting go and just letting everything drop away?

Yes, although the idea of letting go needs to be understood in the right way. It is not about relinquishing possessions, achievements, relationships, or reputation. It is not even about relinquishing thoughts and negative emotions. It is about awareness letting go of its identification with all these things and primarily with the sense of 'I' behind them. When that happens, everything drops away by itself. You don't actually let them go. They drop away of their own accord because there is no longer any identification holding them.

Nisargadatta said it beautifully: "The world is made of rings. The hooks are all yours. Unbend your hooks." But he was not talking to the four lower centers when he said this. He was talking to awareness.

Isn't letting go as you describe it one of the goals of meditation?

This is a good question to explore. What is meditation and what is the goal of meditation?

We might say that the goal is to sweep the mind clear of thoughts, or to open a valve so the stream of thoughts can drain out. On the other hand, we can say the goal is to watch thoughts and in doing so create an inner atmosphere that encourages awareness to realize itself. It is also true that meditation can have all these goals at the same time.

But we have to remember that awareness is not in the four centers. It is above them. It is a different dimension, and the four centers cannot engage that dimension directly. Only awareness can control itself. At best, the four centers can lessen their resistance and provide a welcome environment for awareness. This is what meditation is meant to do for the intellectual center. It is also what yoga is meant to do for the moving center, what prayer is meant to do for the emotional center, and what things like chanting and drumming are meant to do for the instinctive center. These different techniques are tailored to remove the residue of identification in each center. They all have their origin in the idea of purification and surrender. Their purpose is to provide a way for each center to become a clear vessel in which awareness can gather itself, and through which it can realize itself as awareness. When this is understood, these techniques can be very powerful.

Meanwhile, it is important to understand that awareness itself does not meditate or assume postures or pray or chant. It is simply aware of these as they take place. If and when the centers become sufficiently neutralized and empty, awareness can realize itself in their void. But when that happens, you still need to recognize the difference between awareness and the effect that its presence is having on the lower centers. They are not the same thing. Awareness being aware of its own presence happens in the dimension of awareness. It does not happen in the body or in the mind.

What do you mean by neutralized?

Neutralized means free of the residue of identification. Our lives are usually filled with the momentum of identification in all four centers. Thoughts clutter the mind. Tension accumulates in the body. Our emotions get cloudy and turbulent. Our physiology gets out of whack. A lot of debris collects in the centers and this debris affects the centers themselves, the same way corrupted blood cells affect the vessels they flow through. It takes time for things to neutralize and normalize, and that is the purpose of meditation, yoga, and prayer.

If awareness was fully present on a regular basis, identification would never gather enough momentum to cause any buildup of physical or psychological residue. The centers would exist in a neutral condition as clear conduits. Your life would then become a steady chain of meditation and yoga and prayer and chanting. You would be automatically meditating while waiting for the elevator. You would have a yoga moment each time you put on your socks. You would have a prayer moment when you thought kindly of other people. Your bath or shower would become a sort of chant.

All of these things would happen as a result of awareness being aware, instead of you having to harness them to promote awareness. They would come about because awareness was simply manifesting through the four centers unsullied by identification. There would be no reason to set apart time in your day to practice.

The reason you do set apart time for practice is because the momentum of identification has reestablished itself and needs to be neutralized. So you meditate and pray and do yoga to return to clarity as a vessel for awareness.

Another reason that this is a good topic to explore is because it raises the question: who meditates, who practices asanas, who prays? If awareness is not doing these things, who or what is doing them? Here again the fourth way offers an explanation based on the four centers. The idea is that each center has different parts which operate with different levels of attention. For example, some things you can do without thinking about them, like ride a bike, or speak whole sentences, or laugh, or scratch an itch. Other things require careful attention, such as threading a needle, reading instructions, intuiting another person's needs, or tasting the herbs in your food. And these examples don't even compare to the attention it takes to knowingly promote awareness. That level of attention comes from the very highest part of each of the four centers. These higher parts are like the governors of their domains. They can commandeer the whole of themselves and harness a special effort to turn all attention to the task of enabling awareness.

These higher parts of the centers are mediators between the centers themselves and awareness. In religious vernacular they are the high priests of the temple. In fourth way terminology they are higher 'I's in you which value and want to cultivate awareness. This is who initiates your practice, and in that they are invaluable. But they are not awareness and they do not become awareness.

Earlier you said that when awareness identifies it infuses itself in the four lower centers as their identity. But you also implied that some degree of awareness remains?

It is more accurate to say that the energy of awareness gets appropriated by the lower centers as a sense of ego. The deeper core of awareness does remain intact, but it is no longer aware of itself. It loses consciousness of itself. When it is not conscious of itself, it sits in the theater of the mind watching a film of thoughts that has almost nothing to do with what is happening in front of you right now.

This is why trying to notice what is in your immediate environment is so important. When you do this you open the door so awareness can walk out of the theatre of the mind and back into the world. You are giving awareness a chance, which is the best thing the lower centers can do for awareness.

The core of awareness also remains even when its unconscious energy is spent through negative emotions. The next time a negative emotion takes shape in you, try to notice that awareness realizes it is disappearing into the negative emotion, and that it realizes when it re-emerges from the negative emotion minutes, hours, or days later. In the interim, however, it is completely lost to itself, like the prodigal son on a blind spree.

You have said that art also gives awareness a chance and that certain art forms can be conveyors of awareness. Can you comment?

In general, we can distinguish between art that the ego creates to express itself and art that originates in awareness and consciously serves to evoke awareness in the viewer and listener. You find the latter in the music of Bach, the self-portraits of Rembrandt, and the writings of Shakespeare and Walt Whitman. Their external art transmits an internal silence of truth which resonates in the awareness of the viewer and makes the viewer more conscious.

For centuries people have asked why the arts are valuable and necessary, but they always answer this question in terms of the four lower centers. As a result, art is taught as technique, as a form of personal expression, and as a product while the real answer lies in the miracle that the arts can convey awareness. They can store awareness, transport it through time, and convey it again and again. This is the inexplicable majesty of the finest of the arts.

The arts are also unique because they capture the moment inside a boundary. When you consciously look at and listen to the finest of the arts, you enter into an extended moment that allows awareness to settle and roam inside the boundary of that moment which has been preserved in the art form. In this sense, viewing the arts can revitalize awareness by giving it a means to contain itself and realize itself. This is why visiting a gallery or theatre or concert hall can be so enriching.

Nature has a similar ability to make us more aware.

This is interesting because the form of nature is not man-made whereas the form of the arts is. Flowers, for example, stand out in a room because they are often the only thing in the room that was not given form by mankind. They stand as a delicate reflection of a higher world in this world.

Trees are similar. When you notice trees you realize how special they are and that they, too, are a reflection of a higher dimension. Most trees live longer than we do, and apart from their movement as they grow and bend in the wind, they remain remarkably still and silent. Even in a fallen tree you can sense the stillness that was at the core of its being. It's as though you are seeing the silent spirit of a fallen warrior. Flowers and trees serve as friendly reminders to awareness. When awareness pops out of the soil of body, mind, and ego, it blooms. And even as it continues to expand it remains perfectly silent and still.

Yesterday you said that being conscious of nature is different than being conscious of suffering. Can you please expand on that a little more?

I was talking about what the fourth way calls the two conscious shocks. The first conscious shock refers to self-remembering which means being consciously aware that you are aware of things. The second conscious shock refers to transforming negative emotions and suffering by not identifying with them.

An example of the first shock would be looking at some flowers or a sunset while being aware that you are looking at them. What happens when you are aware like this is that the impression of the flowers or of the sunset comes to you. They surrender themselves to awareness and release themselves into awareness, and awareness embraces them. It consciously receives what it is aware of.

The second conscious shock is different in that awareness is the one who surrenders. You are still consciously aware in the process, but instead of the suffering coming to awareness, awareness consciously yields to the suffering without fighting it. It lets the force of suffering pass through it and, in effect, give its energy to awareness. This cannot happen unconsciously. It has to be a conscious transformation.

So when you look at nature, let nature come into awareness. And when you face suffering, allow the suffering to pass through awareness. In both cases, awareness remains empty and gentle as it is filled up and transformed.

Why are they called conscious shocks?

This is an entire subject unto itself, but for now I can say that they are called conscious shocks because they don't happen unconsciously. When awareness is unaware of being aware, then what I just described happens in the opposite way. Instead of the impressions of the world coming to us, we go after them. We grasp them physically and psychologically. Notice, for instance, how hard you look at things. Awareness goes into them instead of them coming into conscious awareness.

And in terms of suffering, instead of surrendering to it and letting the force of its energy pass through us, we usually fight it, resist it, complain about it, and feel sorry for ourselves about it. Instead of the suffering serving as fuel for conscious awareness, we fuel the suffering by identifying with it and expressing negative emotions about it. There is nothing conscious going on. When we identify with suffering, one of our biggest opportunities for transformation is lost and we don't even realize it.

I struggle with identification and I know I am struggling, but I cannot stop it or get out if it. Then I just get more frustrated.

This is because we cannot struggle with identification as long as we are identified. Struggling implies identification. It means that we have become identified with the fact that we are identified. It means we are inside identification trying to work on identification.

A good example of this is fear. We feel afraid and we either become afraid of the fear or we try to fight it. Yet there are really three things going on. First there is the sensation of fear. Second there is the feeling of being a person who is afraid. Third is the awareness that sees the first two. Because of identification, most of our energy goes into the first two which we experience as one because they unfold so fast.

What would be preferable is to go in the other direction, toward awareness and into awareness. Awareness being aware of being aware as it perceives is a fourth element, the fourth dimension. When this dimension opens up, the thing we call fear and the person we call 'me' feeling afraid start to look different.

Fear is a good example because it is fueled by adrenal intensity in the instinctive center which insists that we not only be afraid but that we be afraid of the fear. This intensity quickly spirals into the other three centers and all we know is panic. When you feel this happening, try to distinguish between the instinctive sensation of fear, the emotional obligation to be afraid of it, and the intensity of energy fueling both. Then try to be aware that you are aware of all of them. This thing we call fear may continue, but you will be out of it watching it. It will not drown you as before.

I notice I just get pulled in. I get identified right away and right away I am negative. But it is with anger, not fear. Things get in my way and I get angry.

The more you are identified, the more you feel it as it courses through your lower centers. It is like an electric current that makes you excited, anxious, fearful, aggressive, angry, and so on, depending on the situation and the makeup of your ego.

The electric charge of identification also opens the psychological storehouse of negative emotions and releases them as weapons and defense mechanisms. The ego keeps them at the ready to deploy whenever it encounters situations it doesn't like.

Without identification, negative emotions cannot accumulate and the ego cannot grow. The reverse is also true. The more you get angry, the more angry you will be able to get each time after that. In your case, it sounds like anger is your go-to negative emotion for dealing with things you perceive as obstacles. Try to lay down this weapon for awhile and see what happens. You may be surprised. The ego will feel helpless at first. See if you can move past that and align yourself with awareness.

I agree, but how do I turn off the impulse that causes me to pick up the weapon in the first place?

Try to notice that there are three aspects to your reaction. There is the point where it begins, there is the flow of energy passing through you, and there is the point where it ends. When we first learn about identification, we usually mistake the end point, which is the *result* of identification, for the flow of identification itself. We think we are hurrying because the moving center is identified, or that we are frustrated with an idea because the intellectual center is identified, or that we are in a bad mood because the instinctive and emotional centers are identified. We then try to change those results or make them go away. We try to control our excitement or rein in our aggression, or calm our anxiety. In other words, we try to address identification at its end point in terms of how it has affected the lower centers.

Alternatively, as you start to recognize the current of identification flowing through you, you try to stop it, turn it off, or somehow shake it off. But then you discover that once the flow has started it cannot be turned off midstream. The only way to turn identification off is at the spicket, the point where it starts.

This brings you to the realization that identification is not about the lower centers. They are just receptacles for it. You see that identification is about the flow of unconscious awareness. When awareness is unconscious, its chemical makeup changes in such a way that it attaches itself to whatever it flows toward. On the other hand, when awareness remains conscious of itself, it maintains awareness at its source, while it is flowing, and as it reaches whatever it is perceiving. All three become one thing and remain as the same awareness. When you understand this, you will see how to stop identification at its source, before it starts.

Another tip is to not think of it as *your* anger. Don't say, 'I am angry.' Simply see it as a surge of intense energy inside you. Peel away the word 'anger' and your ownership of it. See it as an entity unto itself. Then ask yourself if you really want to keep living with it. Look carefully and you will see that deep down something in you wants to live with the anger and is choosing to live with it, to allow it.

It is a beautiful thing when you see this. It means you have cracked the armor of the ego and that you are peering through the crack.

Earlier you said there are two stages of identification? Now it sounds like there are three. Is that right?

What I mentioned earlier were the stages as Ouspensky described them: one where identification is beginning and one where it is complete. Both of these stages refer to when identification is flowing through you. The starting and end points I mentioned are something different. The starting point means pure awareness before it becomes identification. The end point means the effect after identification has penetrated the lower centers.

Near the starting point, awareness is conscious and can catch identification before it starts. The airplane is taxiing but you can stop it before it reaches the runway. When awareness is less conscious, the plane is already on the runway or starting to take flight. Sometimes you can stop the plane at the end of the runway or force it to turn around and land after it has taken off. But this has to happen right at the beginning. Otherwise it is too late because the airplane is in full flight. Identification has already gained altitude.

The airplane of identification of course never lands. It always crashes as extreme behavior or the expression of negative emotions, and often the best awareness can do is realize that it has crashed. But rather than trying to sort out the mess at the crash sight, which is what psychotherapy does, awareness has the option to return immediately to the starting point and reestablish itself as pure awareness. This is the prodigal son returning home at the same instant that he realizes the error of his ways. He did not try to rectify his debauchery. He went straight to his father's house. Awareness was lost and immediately found itself reunited with its source.

It feels like the temptation to be identified is everywhere in my life. It also feels like it gives me energy. Is that always a bad thing?

This temptation is everywhere because the mind and body are poised to allow identification. Their potential for facilitating identification is inherent in our bloodstream. It is no small thing to swim against this stream. It means transcending a cosmic law that is as powerful if not more powerful than gravity. It means trying to reach the point where awareness is free to expand as itself rather than be compressed in human form.

The more you investigate identification, the more you see that it is not about what you are identified with. It is about identity. When we are identified, we have identity. When we are not identified, we have no identity. There is simply awareness. The body and mind are then a clear conduit with no 'me' attached to it.

Try to understand that you the person are not identified. Awareness is what gets identified, and when it does it creates a sense of you as a body, name, nationality, and so on. We are loathe to give this up because the ego likes the feeling of security that comes with identity, despite the suffering it causes us.

Breaking the bond of identification is not about you the person being less identified and feeling better. It is about awareness realizing itself as awareness and slipping out of the notion of being a person.

In my case, I get identified with thoughts and cannot let go. It feels like I am glued to the search for finding answers.

This is a good description of the greed and determination of the mind. The mind is a grasper. It is always trying to grasp for an opinion, a conclusion, an analysis, or a refutation. It is desperate to pin things down and keep them in its clutches. But this clutching is exactly what binds awareness. Jean Klein said that thought is a contraction, the same way a muscle contracts. When our mind thinks, it usually contracts because we are identified, and this contraction goes against the relaxed openness of awareness. But the mind doesn't have to do this. We can relax it when we think, and our thinking will be better for it.

Jean Klein suggested trying to feel the brain inside the skull while also feeling the eyes and the orbital nerve connecting them to the brain. This by itself can bring you to clearer awareness and better thinking. The trouble is never our thoughts. It is the tendency of awareness to plunge into them with identification and lose itself in their current.

Another thing you can try is to slow down your speech and allow for pauses between thoughts when you are talking. People are talking faster and faster these days, with fewer pauses between thoughts. There is more compulsion behind speech, almost frenzy. And people don't realize that the stronger the compulsion, the less chance there is for awareness to surface and breathe.

Jean Klein also made the observation that thinking is usually a defense mechanism of the ego; a guarded reaction. You can see this in the impulse to immediately throw up a thought or opinion when you read or hear something or listen to someone. Instead of absorbing what is coming in, we block it by reacting with thought. Likewise, when we have the chance to speak in turn, our thoughts are often forward-charging and offensive as well as defensive. The ego basically wants to prove to itself and to others that its thinking is right. Real thinking has greater depth than that. It does not force or persuade or protect. It explores. It discovers. It reveals. At its best it carves new pathways for awareness to flow through.

These things called thoughts are a curious phenomenon. They emerge from the void, affect our outlook, recede into the void, and then come around again and again, like comets in mental space.

Is there a connection between identification and chief feature?

Chief feature is the electrode. Ego is the strip of wire wrapped around it. Together they enable the charge of identification to flow with ease through the lower centers. The combined effect produces what we experience as a sharpened sense of identity. We feel more distinct when we are identified, but it is an illusion.

The idea of an electrical conductor and wire may also apply to the earth and the thin strip of organic life on its surface. According to the fourth way, this strip of organic life enables a particular kind of charge to flow through the earth and pass influences from the sun and planets to the moon. The idea is that the earth cannot do this by itself because it lacks sufficient conductivity which the layer of organic life on its surface provides. The fourth way explanation is that this is why organic life exists on the earth, so that planetary influences can be transmitted to the earth and digested in a certain way before being passed to the moon.

We also don't know of other planets constructed this way. As far as science can tell, the other planets have no outer strip made of a different material. The closest possibility may be the rings of Saturn which have a composition different than that of their parent planet. This is just a supposition, but it is interesting that certain influences cannot penetrate Saturn without first passing through its rings.

You said that plants and animals don't have egos? So they don't have this wire wrapped around them?

That's right. Energy flows through them, animates them, and gives them tangible presence, but their sense of aliveness is tied strictly to their instinctive core. Although they may have a certain character, such as with dogs, there is no intellectual center, no established emotional center, and no ego. These additional layers in the human psyche provide a finer and more nuanced charge of energy. In this sense, human beings are the most sophisticated receptacle on the surface of the earth.

This also relates to the fourth way idea that just as each person is a receptacle and transmitter of influences, so are the earth, the solar system, the galaxy, the universe, and whatever the universe may be part of. One large conductor comprises a series of smaller and smaller conductors. Together they form a whole whose consciousness is awareness.

Is our ego in the body or in the mind, or in both?

It is mainly in the mind. It forms out of the contents of the mind, out of the same material that comprises thoughts. When the mind is empty, there is no ego. When it fills up with thoughts it becomes the ego. You might say that the ego repeatedly assembles the image of itself in the mind. This is why I call it a hologram because it does not exist except as a mental image that takes on different shapes but always on the same psychological foundation. It even talks to itself in the form of thoughts having a conversation with each other. It says, "This is me" and "This is my body." "I have a wonderful mind." "I have a terrible body." "Well, it isn't that terrible, and you aren't that smart." "I would really like a cheeseburger right now." "You better not."

We are so accustomed to this internal dialogue that we don't realize it is happening. We give too much credence to thoughts, emotions, and sensations, and not enough credence to the awareness looming behind them. We need to turn around and look at awareness itself. When we do, we discover awareness looking back, and discover that it is looking at itself.

Does the ego dissolve all at once and leave just an empty mind?

Some people have it described it that way, though it is not the only experience. For instance, you may transcend the underlying sense of 'I' for a period of time and think it is gone. Then it creeps back in as innocent thoughts, or tries to overwhelm awareness with concerns and problems. In both cases it tries to persuade awareness that it is the real deal, the real you. It is a test of the best kind. Each time you pass the test, awareness gets stronger and the ego loses its strength. The hologram fades away.

Does the ego determine chief feature or grow out of chief feature?

You are not born with an ego, but you are born with the rudiments of a chief feature. You can see this in small children who exhibit a lot of power or destructiveness, or who have a strong tendency to show off or be withdrawn. They exhibit signs of a pure feature without an ego. As the child develops, the ego gradually forms around chief feature and takes on its flavor. It also takes on the attitudes and behavior that you absorb from family, friends, education, culture, religion, and career.

This is why professionals often have a similar flavor of ego. Instead of being themselves, they adopt the characteristics of their profession which manifest through their attitudes, behavior, and dress. You see this with professors, policemen, priests, truck drivers, lawyers, and more. There are many examples.

Can you say more about the ego wrapping itself around chief feature?

The ego is a byproduct of identification. If you never became identified, there would be no material that could accumulate as the ego. When you do become identified, this material accumulates. In the analogy of an electrical conductor, it gathers around chief feature, provides insulation for it, and lends identity to it which makes it easier for you to become identified and stay identified. The ego spawns negative emotions as a psychological paste to help the ego stick to chief feature. From this description you can see what it might mean if you had no negative emotions and no ego.

Chief feature would still be there as a tendency but it would be impotent as an identity. What happens instead is that we identify over and over again which reinforces negative emotions and fortifies the ego. As I mentioned earlier, this is the resurgence of what Eckhart Tolle calls the pain body. The more often it resurges, the more it solidifies and calcifies and becomes harder to shake off.

What exactly is chief feature? I mean as a thing, as a psychological entity?

It is an intriguing question, but we cannot see chief feature or the ego that way. What we can see is the behavior they produce and the kinds of attitudes they adhere to. If you go deep enough, you can also feel the energy behind them. Like a vibration. Each feature and its companion ego has a certain vibration, a psychological flavor that you can almost taste.

Often without knowing it, we will feel the vibration of someone else's chief feature and if it doesn't resonate with the vibration of our own we feel irritated by them. If it does resonate, we like the other person. In either case we don't decide. Chief feature decides.

This Mystery and I

You said negative emotions are essentially the same as far as how they operate. I don't see how anger and depression are the same. Or fear and resentment.

Negative emotions such as anger, fear, and violence operate with high voltage and low amps whereas suspicion, jealousy, and resentment operate with low voltage and high amps. The former explode out of you or erupt inside you. The latter seep out or slowly corrode within. In all these cases, the energy of identification remains the same. It simply manifests in different ways through different kinds of features and variations of ego.

My negative emotions feel like a civil war. I feel like I am always fighting against myself and with the turmoil in myself.

Some people are constantly at war with themselves. Others are battling other people, their circumstances, and the world. Whether the war takes place inside or outside, it involves blaming, criticizing, complaining, and trying to set things right according to our view of what right means. Nations do the same thing. Just as negative emotions lie at the center of the ego, war lies at the center of humanity. It is only a difference of scale. Each nation even displays the characteristics of a chief feature and ego.

According to the fourth way, the characteristics we find in chief feature are the result of planetary influences acting on humanity. In this sense, we do not function independently here on earth. Both individually and collectively, we are governed by planetary influences. Everything in the solar system is connected in ways we don't normally see. The sun, the planets, the earth, humanity, and the moon are all interconnected. This changes the picture considerably.

But we are so small and insignificant.

A single individual is almost insignificant in humanity. Humanity is almost insignificant in the solar system, which is almost insignificant in the galaxy, which in turn is almost insignificant in the universe. Almost. Which means that each world is still big enough to be affected by the influences of much bigger worlds.

Despite these enormous differences of scale in the solar system and galaxy, isn't it remarkable how multifaceted and intricate organic life on earth is? There is something unique about our existence here on earth in the form of human beings. For instance, just the fact that we can perceive this and be here talking about it is remarkable. Do you suppose the planets and galaxies have conversations like this?

Sometimes I feel the larger scheme of the universe when I walk in nature.

Whenever you go on a walk in the country or in the city, try to look at the earth and humanity around you as though you don't exist. The more you take yourself as a person out of the picture, the more awareness comes into focus and the more you start to see a larger view of reality. The more you start to experience the mystery of pure awareness.

Within this larger view of reality, what is the meaning of life?

David Hawkins once said that everything already is what it means. This is a beautifully simple way to look at the world. A pebble already is what it means. So is a trash can and a molecule. It can be enough just to look at everything this way.

The mind can never know the meaning or purpose of life, but awareness can perceive it. This is what David Hawkins was pointing to. We might also say that the purpose of life is to live, and the meaning of life is to know you are living and to realize that you realize that. This is as far as the mind can go. Beyond that there is only awareness which is its own meaning and purpose.

But we still have to live a life?

Yes. And the more awareness we bring to living, the more precious life becomes. But you have to remember that when we say our life what we really mean is the four lower centers operating in the physical and psychological realms of a human on earth. The lower centers are like our life in the city, while awareness sits in a tower above the city with a very different perspective. You still go about the business of living your life in the city, but it now includes the view from the tower and this changes how you live. In effect, as you live you also watch yourself living. Or, it is better to say that as you live the life of a person, awareness watches you live and is conscious of itself watching.

You can also think of awareness as the sky surrounding all the activity of your life on earth. When you are identified, the sky falls. It collapses out of itself and onto the earth. It becomes the earth, just as awareness becomes the person when it identifies with the four lower centers. When it remembers to be aware, it rises again. It ascends to heaven.

I would like to hear more about what awareness itself is and how to recognize it. You say the mind and body want to interpret it on their terms, but that it is beyond them. What exactly is beyond them?

(extended pause…)

The body is a source of movement. The mind is a source of thought. The ego is a source of identity. Awareness is the source of itself. It cannot be seen by anything it sees because compared to everything else it is a void. It cannot even see itself because it has no form. If it had to be described in bodily terms it would be an infinite omnidirectional eye and nothing else. But even this analogy falls short of conveying the nature of awareness. It sounds too simple, but awareness is what knows itself as the awareness that is aware of everything else.

The reason the lower centers cannot understand awareness is because it is not an 'I', a who, or an identity. It has no form, does not dwell in time, and does not occupy space. All of these things come into existence inside the arena of awareness which is not even an arena because it is not a place and it has no borders.

The lower centers also expect enlightenment to be a tangible experience for them, yet the consciousness of awareness is not something you achieve as a person. It is a dimension you enter as awareness. More accurately, it is the dimension that awareness starts to recognize as itself, and it keeps realizing itself in higher and higher dimensions of itself. When you peel away the word 'awareness' you find an infinite void of pure consciousness that keeps expanding. The more it expands, the more it becomes aware. And the more it becomes aware, the more it expands.

(silent pause...)

As long as awareness is tied to a sense of 'me', the veil remains intact and the view restricted. At the same time, the life form of a human being is remarkable because awareness can flow through this form and consciously realize itself as it does. This is an enormous occurrence in the universe and no other life form on earth appears to have this capacity, nor do we know if it exists elsewhere in the universe. Perhaps it does but in some other way, through some other form or process. That seems probable, but we don't know.

What does seem true is that there is one vast awareness originating from a single source and peering through the eyes of all living creatures. This awareness behind everything is not divided in any way. It is the same awareness. The only distinction between life forms is the degree to which this awareness is aware of itself perceiving through them. In this sense we do not have awareness. Awareness has us. Even our life is not for us as the person. It is a catalyst for awareness to consciously realize itself. We are not passing through our life. Our life is passing through awareness.

Whatever you are doing, the only question is whether awareness is consciously perceiving as you do it. Everything we become, achieve, and accumulate as a person will vanish completely. The only thing that endures is conscious awareness, and the greatest mystery of all is the origin of this awareness and the source of its origin. Yet only awareness is capable of peering into the deep, silent void of its origin and the source of its origin, both of which, paradoxically, are itself.

(silent pause…)

Ultimately everything collapses into awareness and resolves as awareness. But the mind cannot fathom the reality that awareness is everything and everything is awareness. Descriptions such as precious and sacred and mysterious can never do justice to the profound depth and vastness of what lies behind the word awareness.

(silent pause…)

Awareness also realizes that it is the essential substance of the universe. These are words trying to describe it without ever being able to because this substance is not tangible to the body or mind. It is not even tangible to itself, yet it realizes that it is perceptible to an even higher dimension of itself, and it knows that it is somehow folding and unfolding as that. Knowing this, it keeps peering as consciously as it can into itself.

Can you talk about your background and how you came to know about all this?

In 1976 I joined a fourth way school called the Fellowship of Friends led by Robert Burton. We studied the system that Gurdjieff and Ouspensky introduced in the twentieth century. I was a member for more than 30 years.

At a certain point I became interested in the ideas of non-dualism and I left the Fellowship and started studying the teachings of Nisargadatta, Ramana Maharshi, H.W.L. Poonja, Jean Klein, and others. I saw a direct correlation between their ideas and all that I had learned about the fourth way, and I began incorporating the two approaches.

Why did you leave the Fellowship of Friends?

It started becoming clear that awakening had never been about me as a person. The realization came that awareness itself never joins a school, is never in a school, and never leaves a school even though the person may need to be in a school to gain this understanding.

Another factor was a growing perception about my relationship to the teacher. I began to realize that there were actually four of us: me, him, the awareness in me, and the awareness in him. I understood that the true relationship is between awareness and awareness which is the same in each of us, and that this is what the environment of a school leads you to.

This all coincided with the fact that the inner dynamics of the Fellowship had been changing over time. The direction and tone were no longer resonating with my understanding and experience, and I left with a combined sense of sorrow, certainty, and gratitude.

Do you think schools and ashrams are necessary for someone seeking enlightenment?

A main component of any spiritual organization is specialized knowledge. For instance, knowledge about the ego, awareness, lower centers, identification, negative emotions, and so on. Another component is the direct transmission from someone who has full command of this knowledge as well as experience navigating the maze of the ego. A third component is an environment designed to serve as a cocoon in which the ego can be observed, exposed, and eventually transcended.

The question becomes, do you need a school for these special conditions, or can you create them on your own? Certainly it is a different age we live in now where knowledge can circulate widely through books and the internet. We also see more self-proclaimed teachers, gurus, and individuals who believe they are advanced. And there is a plethora of workshops, seminars, and retreats to attend. But do these provide what schools have traditionally provided?

There is also a fourth element which is important when we talk about schools, and that is the preparedness of the students. In the fourth way this is described as having a 'magnetic center', meaning a level of interest in awakening that draws a person to a school and a school to them. No one is born with a magnetic center. It develops over time from reading, life experiences, searching, and suffering. It takes shape apart from the ego and not everyone develops a magnetic center, specifically one that is not only curious about enlightenment but willing to sacrifice other things for it.

Which raises other questions: What is the state of magnetic centers in the world today? Do all people who show interest in higher consciousness have a fully developed magnetic center? Are they sufficiently ready to make a commitment to self-realization? And can they do so without the traditional environment of a school which may offer intangibles that books, lectures, and retreats cannot provide?

There are people who have never spent time in a school who nonetheless have undergone a full transformation. Are they outliers or is this a new norm? In either case, do schools still serve a purpose? If so, where are they today? What form are they taking? Is the work in schools changing, or are schools no longer necessary? I don't have definitive answers to these questions. But I am watching the horizon for indications.

In your experience, what is the best attitude for a student to have toward a teacher?

Jean Klein said the best relationship is when the teacher does not take the student as a student, and the student does not take the teacher as a teacher; that is, when neither takes the other to be the roles they find themselves in. This also means they do not use each other, knowingly or unknowingly, to reinforce their identities as student and teacher. A student and teacher also don't have to be close friends. That is never a requirement or guarantee of progress. What is required is shared valuation for and understanding about self-realization.

What similarities and differences do you see between the fourth way and non-dualism, and do they each have strengths and weaknesses?

They both explain the same circle with the goal of leading you to the center of it. Whereas the fourth way describes the circle in more detail, non-dualism concentrates right away on bringing the center of the circle into focus.

The breadth of information in the fourth way can be overwhelming; so much so that it may distract you from the center of the circle. A lot of ideas can seem so important that they camouflage the significance at the center. But that is not a weakness of the system. It is a weakness of the mind studying the system.

In contrast, non-dualism is fairly simple and direct: "Go to the center of the circle and stay there." The drawback is with the mind's tendency to assume that it can think its way to the center, which it cannot, and for the ego to presume that it is awareness, which it is not. Only awareness can enter the circle of itself. But the mind is clever and the ego tricky, and it is easy to deceive yourself.

The fourth way also uses precise language to describe the nuances of the ego. For example, it distinguishes between what the ego is at its roots, why it develops in the first place, how it forms, how it manifests psychologically, why it is so difficult to pinpoint, and what it means to transcend it. Non-dualism, on the other hand, speaks in terms of the mind and body, occasionally including the senses.

Another difference is that non-dualism implies that self-realization is a single leap of awareness, whereas the fourth way describes degrees of awareness. For instance, there are some people interested in raising their awareness, there are some in whom awareness is starting to self-realize, some in whom it is realized, and some in whom it is fully transcendent.

The fourth way also includes a cosmology that explains our place in the universe, why humankind exists on earth, what makes the evolution of consciousness possible, how the suffering of humanity ties into this, and more. Non-dualism does not provide a larger framework in the same degree of detail. Non-dualism also does not go into depth about, or put emphasis on, negative emotions, whereas the fourth way gives this a special place. The main idea is that negative emotions are the psychological backbone of the ego and that not expressing them is a way of containing the energy behind the ego and using that energy as a catalyst for the transmutation of awareness. This process is akin to cocooning the caterpillar for the purpose of dissolving its constituent parts and reconstituting them as a butterfly. That is just an analogy, but it describes very well what we mean when talking about the ego, negative emotions, and the self-realization of awareness.

You mentioned that more people are proclaiming themselves as self-realized teachers and gurus. Do you think we are in a special time and that more people are becoming enlightened?

There seems to be a prevailing belief that enlightenment, self-realization, awakening, or whatever you choose to call it, has become more common; that it is easier, faster, and more available than in the past. One of the theories behind this is that humanity is constantly evolving and that we may have reached a tipping point in this evolution. But is it true that hundreds or thousands if not tens of thousands of people have pierced the veil of their ego and experienced the self-realization of awareness?

As we talked about earlier, there is a plethora of knowledge about spiritual awakening and no shortage of people teaching enlightenment. The ideas of awareness, mindfulness, being in the moment, attuning yourself to the universe, pursuing abundance, and so on are in the air and being picked up by people around the world. It seems reasonable to conclude that more people are waking up. But are they? The distinctions between mind, body, ego, and awareness are so subtle that the mind thinks it is awareness. And what better for the ego than to be more self-realized than others?

The ego is more complex than people suppose. Its subterfuges are more deceptive than they realize. It is not so easily transcended by so many people so soon. Awareness itself is so pure and delicate and rarefied that it eludes the mind's grasp, even in someone who sincerely feels they want to reach the height of self-realization. That desire is admirable, but that desire does not awaken. We are also talking about a complete transformation, not of the person we have long believed ourselves to be, but of the seed of awareness in us. Self-realization is a transcendence into a higher dimension of perception that is beyond our identity as a person. There doesn't seem to be evidence of this in large numbers even though there are many people displaying genuine interest in enlightenment.

You said the fourth way contends that the planets influence us so we will pass their influence to the earth and moon. Is that right? Can you say more?

According to the fourth way, the moon is inside the field of the earth, which is inside the field of the solar system, which is inside the galaxy, which is inside the vast network of galaxies, all of which are inside an Absolute that comprises all these dimensions of worlds.

The system frames the universe in this model and calls it the 'ray of creation' while leaving open the possibility that there may be an infinite number of rays of creation. The system also explains that humanity is part of a thin sheath on the surface of the earth which includes the human, animal, vegetable, and mineral kingdoms as well as the oceans and atmosphere, and that all of these together comprise what is called 'organic life on earth' which is distinct from the earth itself.

The idea is that the ray of creation grows as a result of celestial influences passing up and down the ray of creation, transmitted from each world above to the ones below and vice-versa. Humanity is regarded as organic life's most sensitive antenna of reception and its most sophisticated organ of digestion for the influences which pass from the sun and planets to the earth, and from the earth to the moon, with the moon being the end point of growth in the ray of creation. The fourth way regards the moon as an embryonic planet which depends on mother earth for sustenance until it can develop the ability to revolve on its own and eventually give birth to its own moon to ensure the growth of the ray of creation.

You can see from this how elaborate the cosmology of the fourth way is. But to continue, the idea is that humanity plays a key role in providing the moon with the sustenance it needs to grow. This sustenance is delivered in the form of magnetic fields which are released by all living matter at death. In the case of humans, while we are alive we also release a specific kind of energy whenever we become identified, express negative emotions, and do harm to each other—all as part of the process of feeding the moon. If this description seems far-fetched, consider the history of humanity, the centuries of conflict and death, along with the extent to which people become identified and the daily dose of negativity that either drips or spills out of people around the world.

The fourth way explains that this turmoil is inherent to the purpose of organic life on earth. At the same time, it explains that influences need to pass back up the ray of creation to the planets and sun and beyond, and that human beings are a unique vessel for achieving this, which is where the transformation of suffering and the evolution of consciousness come in. The idea is that humans can recognize their place in this scheme, how the scheme serves the downward spiral of the ray of creation, and how it can also serve its ascension.

At the same time, not everyone can participate in this ascent because doing so would upset the balance of organic life on earth. If most people were evolving, the moon would not get fed and the ray of creation could not continue to grow. But awareness realizing itself in a certain number of people is light enough to slip through the network of influences being transmitted down the ray of creation.

This is a lot of information, but it may give you a fresh way to think about what life on earth is about, what the evolution of consciousness entails, and what this has to do with awareness realizing itself—or not—within large numbers of people on earth.

If there is a surge of more people awakening, it would mean, according to the fourth way, that something significant is happening in the ray of creation, specifically within organic life and the transmission of influences between planets, earth, and moon. It is useful to understand that our existence on earth and the possibility of self-realization are parts of a much larger whole of universal forces.

We have been talking for a long while and this feels like a good time to retire to the quiet of awareness. As Rumi said: "A great silence overcomes me, and I wonder why I ever thought to use language."

~ ~ ~

This Mystery and I

This Mystery and I

www.ingramcontent.com/pod-product-compliance
Lightning Source LLC
Chambersburg PA
CBHW030039100526
44590CB00011B/260